♪♪♩ Rhythm & Rhyme

Literacy Time

Authors

Timothy Rasinski, Ph.D.

Karen McGuigan Brothers

Gay Fawcett, Ph.D.

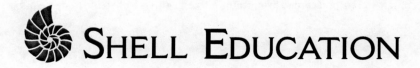

SHELL EDUCATION

Standards

For information on how this resource meets national and other state standards, see pages 137–141. You may also review this information by scanning the QR code or visiting our website at http://www.shelleducation.com and following the on-screen directions.

Publishing Credits

Corinne Burton, M.A.Ed., *President*; Emily R. Smith, M.A.Ed., *Editorial Director*; Jennifer Wilson, *Editor*; Evelyn Garcia, M.A.Ed., *Editor*; Grace Alba, *Multimedia Designer*; Don Tran, *Production Artist*; Amber Goff, *Editorial Assistant*; Stephanie Loureiro, *Assistant Editor*

Image Credits

iStock p. 5, p. 6, p. 19, p. 21, p. 28, p. 35, p. 40, p. 52, p. 60, pp. 74–75, p. 77, p. 79, p. 92, p. 97, pp. 100–101, pp. 108–109, p. 112, p. 116, pp. 128–129, p. 141; all other images Shutterstock

Standards

Shell Education

5301 Oceanus Drive
Huntington Beach, CA 92649-1030
http://www.shelleducation.com

ISBN 978-1-4258-1336-9

© 2015 Shell Educational Publishing, Inc.
Printed in USA. WOR004

Table of Contents

Poetry and Literacy

"Reading should not be presented to children as a chore or duty. It should be offered to them as a precious gift."

—Kate DiCamillo

What better gift to give students than fun rhymes to read in order to build literacy skills? Did you grow up singing a song of sixpence, hoping the kittens would find their mittens, and wondering why Georgie Porgie wouldn't leave those little girls alone? We did, along with generations of children. Mother Goose nursery rhymes have helped children achieve literacy since at least the 18th century. Today, we find that many of our children are missing out on nursery rhymes and poetry. Over the years, poetry and rhymes have been called the "neglected component" and "forgotten genre" in our homes and in our school literacy curricula (Denman 1988; Gill 2011; Perfect 1999). Many teachers think that is a shame, and we heartily agree!

There is a growing chorus of scholars who are advocating the return of poetry and poetry lessons in the classroom (Rasinski, Rupley, and Nichols 2012; Seitz 2013). Moreover, there is a growing body of classroom and clinical research demonstrating the power of poetry in growing readers (Iwasaki, Rasinski, Yildirim, and Zimmerman 2013; Rasinski, Rupley, and Nichols 2008; Zimmerman and Rasinski 2012; Rasinski and Zimmerman 2013; Zimmerman, Rasinski, and Melewski 2013). The following information describes the benefits of using poetry and rhyme to enhance literacy skills in the classroom.

Phonological Awareness

Rhymes provide the context for developing phonological awareness. Dunst, Meter, and Hornby (2011) reviewed twelve studies that examined the relationship between nursery rhymes and emergent literacy skills in more than 5,000 children. All of the studies pointed to a relationship between early knowledge of nursery rhymes and phonological awareness, which is a strong predictor of early reading acquisition (Adams 1990; Ball and Blachman 1991; Griffith and Klesius 1990; Templeton and Bear 2011). In fact, one literacy expert, Keith Stanovich, claims phonological awareness as a predictor of reading success is "better than anything else we know of, including I.Q." (Stanovich 1994, 284). Rhymes provide an opportunity for children to play with words and thus learn how language works (Maclean, Bryant, and Bradley 1987).

Poetry and Literacy *(cont.)*

Phonics

The alliteration of *Goosie Goosie Gander* and the rhyming words of *Jack Sprat Could Eat No Fat* lay the groundwork for phonics instruction. Children can't *sound out* words if they don't hear the sounds. Decades of research have demonstrated that rhymes help children develop an ear for language. In one longitudinal study, researchers found a strong correlation between early knowledge of rhymes in children from ages three to six and success in reading and spelling over the next three years, even when accounting for differences in social background and I.Q. (Bryant, Bradley, Maclean, and Crossland 1989). Poetry and rhymes surround children with the sounds of language—sounds that must be applied in the letter-sound relationships of phonics instruction.

Vocabulary and Comprehension

Even a strong foundation in phonemic awareness and phonics is not enough. Students who can decode words but do not know their meanings usually struggle with comprehension, which is, of course, the ultimate goal of reading. Research has consistently shown a strong correlation between vocabulary and comprehension (Bromley 2007; Chall 1983; National Reading Panel 2000). Typical correlations between standardized measures of vocabulary and reading comprehension are in the .90 or higher range regardless of the measure used or the populations tested (Stahl 2003). Vocabulary development is just one more benefit of using poetry and rhymes with children. Most nursery rhymes present opportunities to learn new vocabulary words that are relevant today but may not be familiar to many five-year-olds (e.g., *kettle* [Polly Put the Kettle On], *buckle* [One, Two, Buckle My Shoe], and *market* [To Market, To Market]).

Fluency

The repeated reading of poems and rhymes provides ample opportunities for students to develop reading fluency. Rasinski and Padak (2013) describe fluency as "a bridge that connects word decoding to comprehension . . . Fluency includes automatic word recognition, interpretive and prosodic reading, and appropriate expression and rate. Fluency is the ability to read expressively and meaningfully, as well as accurately and with appropriate speed" (252). Research into repeated readings indicates that reading a particular passage several times, which we suggest you do with the nursery rhymes and poems in this book, leads not only to fluency with that text but also transfers to new, unfamiliar text (Dowhower 1987, 1997; Rasinski et al. 1994; Samuels 1997; Stahl and Heubach 2005).

> "Purposeful practice is essential for improvement and mastery of literacy skills. When given proper instruction, materials, and opportunities to practice and apply what they learn, all students can experience literacy success" (Hackett 2013, 4).

Poetry and nursery rhymes send the all-important message that reading is fun. What children can resist the tickle in their mouths when they say *Fuzzy Wuzzy* or the onomatopoeia of *Baa Baa Black Sheep*? The natural rhythm and meter beg children to recite nursery rhymes over and over, increasing fluency skills more and more each time. Enjoy watching your students light up as they say each and every one of the rhymes in this book.

How to Use This Book

Implementing the Lessons

The following information explains the various activities in the lessons and how to implement them with students. Additional tips on how to implement the lessons, including creating poetry notebooks, can be found on pages 129–131.

Introducing the Rhyme

This section helps teachers introduce the poems to students. Use the steps listed below to introduce all of the poems in this book. Then, continue with the specific tasks mentioned in each lesson.

1. Copy the rhyme on a sheet of chart paper or on the board, or display a large version on the board.

2. Read the rhyme to students using a pointer to track the print.

3. Distribute copies of the rhyme to students.

4. Read the rhyme chorally several times to develop fluency.

5. Have students illustrate the rhyme and add it to their individual poetry notebooks. For more information about how to set up the poetry notebooks, see page 131.

Change a Word

Some lessons include the *Change a Word* activity. With this activity, students are given letter cards (page 132) that can be arranged to make words from the rhyme. **Note:** Some lessons require duplicate letters. Be sure to look at Step 1 in each *Change a Word* activity and write the additional letters on the empty cards. You can also use the blank cards to quickly create new letter cards for students who accidentally lose one of the letters. You may also wish to laminate them for durability. The first word and the last word will be connected to the poem. Sometimes the activity requires simple encoding (using just a few letters to make a simple CVC word chain for the rhyme "Handy-Spandy, Jack-A-Dandy": *shop, pop, top, mop, hop*). At other times, instructions require students to use the final letter of a word they made to start the next word in the chain (going from *pot* to *pan* for the rhyme "The Fly" by Karen McGuigan Brothers: *pot, top, pup, pan*).

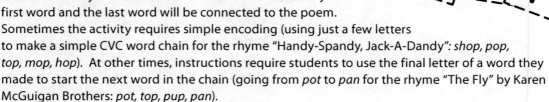

Since this activity is teacher-led (the teacher reads the clues), it should be done as a whole-class activity, or you may wish to work with some students in a small group. Be sure to clarify any clues or word meanings that students may be unfamiliar with. **Note:** You may wish to continue this activity by guiding students in making other words of your choosing with the letter cards.

How to Use This Book (cont.)

Word Ladders

Lessons that do not have a *Change a Word* activity will have a *Word Ladder* activity, which allows students to build and examine words on an activity sheet. To begin, students are given a key word from the rhyme. In order to "climb the ladder," students must follow the teacher's clues and change the first word progressively, thus creating a new word at each step. Clues can require students to add, remove, change, or rearrange letters. The final word relates to the first word. For example, for the rhyme "To Market" students follow your instructions to progressively change the following words: *fat, bat, bit, big, rig, pig*.

Since this activity is teacher-led (the teacher reads the clues), it should be done as a whole-class activity, or you may wish to work with some students in a small group. Be sure to clarify any clues or word meanings that students may be unfamiliar with.

Word Sorts

The *Word Sort* activity helps students explore relationships among words. Students are given a set of picture cards or word cards related to the rhyme and work individually, in pairs, or in groups to sort the cards into two or more categories. Some will be *open* word sorts and some will be *closed*.

For open sorts, the categories are not predetermined. Students look for commonalities among the words and create their groups or categories accordingly. Then, they share their word sorts with classmates, explaining the groups they created. For example, given a set of picture cards (*skates, sandwich, doll, donut*) students could sort the cards by initial sounds (/s/ or /d/) or by function (toys and food). As long as they can justify their groups, the sorting is accepted. **Note:** You may find open word sorts are effective as pre-reading activities. The sorting allows students to become familiar with the words they will encounter in the rhymes. In addition, the sorting can help students predict what the text will be about. If used as a pre-reading activity, you will want to have them sort again after reading the rhyme in order to see if their categories change.

For closed word sorts, the categories are predetermined. The teacher instructs students to sort their words into specified categories. After the sorting, students discuss the words and why they were placed in the given categories. **Note**: For each closed word sort, we suggest categories for sorting the words. You can also come up with other categories for your students to use.

Yes and No

This *Yes and No* activity is also a word-sorting activity, but it is completely teacher led. Using a pile of picture cards, the teacher guides students in determining which pictures are "Yes" because they have something in common. For example, items in the *yes* pile might be the same color, have the same vowel sound, or serve a similar function. All other pictures go into the *no* pile. The goal is for students to determine the rule for why pictures are a "Yes." **Note:** One example for yes and one example for no are given in each lesson plan. You may need to give more examples for each pile before students will be able to determine the rule.

How to Use This Book (cont.)

Rhyming Riddles ???

Each lesson includes a *Rhyming Riddles* activity. Students are instructed to use words in a word bank to answer riddles related to a key word or phrase from the rhyme. Students may be able to do this independently, or it can be conducted as a large group activity. Have students say as many rhyming words as they can to partners before implementing the activity sheets so that students know which rhyming sounds they are focusing on. You may wish to have them use the *My Rhyming Words* template (page 133) to write all of the rhyming words they brainstorm.

Writing Connections 📝

Each lesson includes a *Writing Connection* activity that relates to the rhyme in some way. The activities vary from students writing short, one-syllable words, to writing simple poems, to making lists. We suggest that you use these lessons to generate enjoyment of writing rather than to teach grammar and spelling. For the younger students, encourage developmental spelling, dictation, and illustrations, and celebrate your young writers' products. **Note**: Have writing paper available for the *Writing Connection* in all lessons.

Reader's Theater 🎭

Each lesson includes a *Reader's Theater* script that focuses on the rhyme, where students are assigned parts of a script to read aloud. Oral language fluency is an important precursor to oral reading fluency. Fluent speakers actually help their listeners make sense of words and ideas by speaking at an appropriate pace, using meaningful phrases, and embedding expression and pauses into their speech—essentially the same skills needed for fluent reading (Rasinski and Padak 2013).

Have students rehearse the poem several times by themselves or in small groups to enhance listening and speaking skills and improve students' confidence. Arrange for various ways that students can then perform the poem as well as the accompanying script. Students can perform for classmates, another class, parents, the school principal, other teachers, or even record their reading for later performance. **Note**: There are not enough parts for every student in your class. Be sure to look over the amount of parts before assigning them to students.

All of the scripts provide opportunities for repeated reading, the benefits of which we discussed above. Rasinski and Padak (2013) call it "deep reading" (5) and suggest the following routine: "I'll read it to you. You read it with me. Now you read it alone" (66). The problem teachers sometimes face with repeated reading, particularly with older students, is motivating students to read a text multiple times. As one solution to that dilemma, each lesson has a suggestion for tying the repeated reading to a performance. Students should not be required to memorize the text for the performance but simply be prepared to read it aloud with confidence and with good expression.

Row, Row, Row Your Boat

Standards

- Determine or clarify the meaning of unknown and multiple-meaning words and phrases based on kindergarten reading and content.
- Blend and segment onsets and rimes of single-syllable spoken words.
- See Appendix C for additional standards.

Materials

- *Row, Row, Row Your Boat* (page 11)
- *Letter Cards* (page 132)
- *Row, Row, Row Your Boat Yes and No Sort* (pages 12–13)
- *Row, Row, Row Your Boat Rhyming Riddles* (page 14)
- *Row, Row, Row Your Boat Reader's Theater* (page 15)
- chart paper

Procedures

Introducing the Rhyme

1. Copy the rhyme onto a sheet of chart paper.
2. Read the rhyme to students using a pointer to track print.
3. Discuss the words *row*, *stream*, *gently*, and *merrily* from the rhyme.
4. Discuss with students what the line, *Life is but a dream* means.
5. Distribute the *Row, Row, Row Your Boat* rhyme (page 11) to students.
6. Read the rhyme chorally several times to develop fluency.
7. Allow students to illustrate the rhyme and add it to their individual poetry notebooks.
8. Have students add the title to their notebooks' tables of contents.

Change a Word

1. Distribute a set of *Letter Cards* (page 132) to each student. If this activity is used early in the year, we recommend you use only the letters they will need (*b, o, a, t, g, c*).
2. Before you begin to play, have students identify the letters and corresponding sounds.
3. Allow students time to arrange the letters to make their own words.
4. After students have had time to make and share words, ask them to put the letters in a pile and follow your instructions to make a word chain from *boat* to *boat* (*boat-oat-goat-coat-boat*). Say the following:
   - We are going to make rhyming words.
   - Think of the word *boat* in the rhyme. Make the word *boat* with your letters.
   - Take off the letter *b*. What word do you have now? (*oat*)
   - Add the letter *g* at the front. What word do you have now? (*goat*)
   - Take off the letter *g* and put the letter *c* in its place. What word do you have now? (*coat*)
   - Take off the letter *c* and put the letter *b* in its place. What word do you have now? (*boat*)
   - What did you notice about the word we started and ended with?

Row, Row, Row Your Boat *(cont.)*

Yes and No Sort

1. Make a copy of the *Row, Row, Row Your Boat Yes and No Sort* cards (pages 12–13).

2. Have students sit on the floor in a circle. Say, "We will make two piles of pictures in the middle of the circle. One will be the *yes* pile and one will be the *no* pile. Your job is to figure out why a word is a *yes* or a *no*. When you figure out the rule that makes the words *yes* or *no*, don't say it until I ask you to."

3. Hold up the *car* card for students to see. Tell them that the card belongs in the *yes* pile.

4. Hold up the *hat* card for students to see. Tell them that the card belongs in the *no* pile.

5. Have students sort the remaining cards into the *yes* or *no* piles.

6. Ask students for the rule (something to ride in).

Rhyming Riddles ???

1. Ask students to think of words that rhyme with the word *row*. Have them share their words with partners.

2. Record their words on the board.

3. Distribute *Row, Row, Row Your Boat Rhyming Riddles* (page 14) to students and make connections between the words that students come up with in Step 1 to the words in the Word Bank.

4. Instruct students to use words from the Word Bank to complete the riddles.

5. Have students illustrate one of the rhyming riddles on the backs of their papers.

Writing Connection

1. Divide students into pairs.

2. Have students work with partners to create lists of things to ride in. Encourage developmental spelling.

3. Have students share their lists. Keep track of how many different forms of transportation were identified.

Reader's Theater

1. Distribute the *Row, Row, Row Your Boat Reader's Theater* script (page 15) to students.

2. Read the script together.

3. Divide the class into four groups, and assign each group a part.

4. Allow several rehearsals to develop fluency.

5. To encourage students to track print, create sentence strips, reorder the lines, and read the rhyme as indicated.

6. Perform the reader's theater for the class, another class, or for a special school event.

Row, Row, Row Your Boat

Traditional Rhyme

Row, row, row your boat

Gently down the stream.

Merrily, merrily, merrily, merrily,

Life is but a dream.

Row, Row, Row Your Boat
Yes and No Sort

Directions: Cut apart the cards. Then, sort them into two groups: a *Yes* pile and a *No* pile.

Row, Row, Row Your Boat

Yes and No Sort (cont.)

Name: _____

Row, Row, Row Your Boat

Rhyming Riddles

. . . .

Directions: Use words from the Word Bank to complete the riddles about rowing.

Word Bank

- -

| mow | snow | crow | low |

- -

1. row in the wintertime

_____

– – – – – – – – – –

row in the _____

2. row with a black bird

_____

– – – – – – – – – –

row with a _____

3. row in deep grass

_____

– – – – – – – – – –

row where you need to _____

4. row deep down

_____

– – – – – – – – – –

row _____

Row, Row, Row Your Boat
Reader's Theater

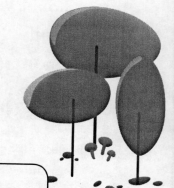

All: Row, Row, Row Your Boat

Group 1: Row, row, row your boat

Group 2: Gently down the stream.

Group 3: Merrily, merrily, merrily, merrily,

Group 4: Life is but a dream.

All: Row, row, row your boat

Group 1: Merrily, merrily, merrily, merrily,

Group 2: Gently down the stream.

Group 3: Row, row, row your boat

Group 4: Life is but a dream.

Polly, Put the Kettle On

Standards

◎ Demonstrate basic knowledge of one-to-one letter-sound correspondences by producing the primary or many of the most frequent sounds for each consonant.

◎ Count, pronounce, blend, and segment syllables in spoken words.

◎ See Appendix C for additional standards.

Materials

◎ *Polly, Put the Kettle On* (page 18)

◎ *Letter Cards* (page 132)

◎ *Polly, Put the Kettle On Closed Word Sort* (pages 19–20)

◎ *Polly, Put the Kettle On Rhyming Riddles* (page 21)

◎ *Polly, Put the Kettle On Reader's Theater* (page 22)

◎ chart paper

Procedures

Introducing the Rhyme

1. Copy the rhyme onto a sheet of chart paper.

2. Read the rhyme to students using a pointer to track print.

3. Discuss the following questions with students:

   ◎ What do you think a *kettle* is? How do you know?

   ◎ Who will fix the tea for them?

   ◎ Who do you think will come for tea?

   ◎ Who is going to take the kettle off? Why?

   ◎ Where do you think everyone went?

4. Read the rhyme again, pointing to individual words. Ask students to pat their knees and identify how many syllables they hear.

5. Distribute the *Polly, Put the Kettle On* rhyme (page 18) to students.

6. Read the rhyme chorally several times to develop fluency.

7. Ask students to circle the letters that make the sounds /p/ and /s/.

8. Allow students to illustrate the rhyme and add it to their individual poetry notebooks.

9. Have students add the title to their notebooks' tables of contents.

Change a Word

1. Distribute a set of *Letter Cards* (page 132) to each student. If this activity is used early in the year, we recommend you use only the letters they will need (*o, l, l, l, y, j, p, g, h, d, f, m*).

2. Before you begin the activity, have students identify the letters and corresponding sounds.

3. Allow students time to arrange the letters to make their own words.

4. After students have had time to make and share words, ask them to put the letters in a pile and follow your instructions to make rhyming words. Say the following:

   ◎ Who in the rhyme was going to make tea? (*polly*)

   ◎ Find the letter in your pile that starts Polly's name. (*p*)

   ◎ Look at the rhyme on the chart and use the letters you need to finish her name.

   ◎ What letters did you use? (*p, o, l, l, y*)

   ◎ Take off the *p* and put a *j* at the front. What word did you make? (*jolly*)

5. Continue replacing the initial letter to make the rhyming words *jolly, golly, holly, dolly, folly, lolly,* and *molly*. Discuss the meaning of each word as it is made.

Polly, Put the Kettle On (cont.)

Closed Word Sort

1. Distribute the *Polly, Put the Kettle On Closed Word Sort* cards (pages 19–20). Students should have their own sets.

2. Have students sit on the floor in a circle. Say, "We will make two piles of pictures in the middle of the circle. One pile will be pictures that begin with the /s/ sound, and the other pile will be pictures that begin with the /p/ sound."

3. Hold up the *pot* card for students to see. Tell them that the card belongs in the /p/ pile.

4. Hold up the *sun* card for students to see. Tell them that the card belongs in the /s/ pile.

5. Have students continue sorting the cards into the correct piles.

Rhyming Riddles

1. Ask students to think of words that rhyme with the word *tea*. Have them share their words with partners.

2. Record their words on the board.

3. Distribute *Polly, Put the Kettle On Rhyming Riddles* (page 21) to students and make connections between the words that students come up with in Step 1 to the words in the Word Bank.

4. Instruct students to use words from the Word Bank to complete the riddles.

5. Have students illustrate one of the rhyming riddles on the backs of their papers.

Writing Connection

1. Have students write words that begin with the /s/ and /p/ sounds. Encourage everything from scribbles, to single words, to developmental spelling of sentences.

2. Have students share their words with the class. Celebrate all attempts at writing.

Reader's Theater

1. Distribute the *Polly, Put the Kettle On Reader's Theater* script (page 22) to students.

2. Read the rhyme together.

3. Divide the class into two groups, and assign each group a stanza.

4. Allow several rehearsals to develop fluency.

5. Perform the reader's theater for the class, another class, or for a special school event.

Polly, Put the Kettle On

Traditional Rhyme

Polly, put the kettle on,

Polly, put the kettle on,

Polly, put the kettle on,

And we'll all have tea.

Sukey, take it off again,

Sukey, take it off again,

Sukey, take it off again,

They're all gone away.

Polly, Put the Kettle On

Closed Word Sort

Directions: Cut apart the cards. Then, sort them into two groups: words that start with the letter *s* and words that start with the letter *p*.

Polly, Put the Kettle On

Closed Word Sort (cont.)

Name: _____

Polly, Put the Kettle On
Rhyming Riddles

Directions: Use words from the Word Bank to complete the riddles about Polly.

Word Bank

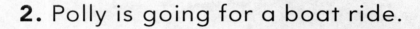

bee   tea   knee   sea

1. Polly is having a drink.

_____

Polly is having _____.

2. Polly is going for a boat ride.

_____

Polly is going to _____.

3. Polly got stung.

_____

Polly stepped on a _____.

4. Polly fell down.

_____

Polly scraped her _____.

Polly, Put the Kettle On

Reader's Theater

All: Polly, Put the Kettle On

Group 1: Polly, put the kettle on,

Polly, put the kettle on,

Polly, put the kettle on,

All: And we'll all have tea.

Group 2: Sukey, take it off again,

Sukey, take it off again,

Sukey, take it off again,

All: They're all gone away.

Baa, Baa, Black Sheep

Standards

- Determine or clarify the meaning of unknown and multiple-meaning words and phrases based on kindergarten reading and content.

- Add or substitute individual sounds (phonemes) in simple, one-syllable words to make new words.

- See Appendix C for additional standards.

Materials

- *Baa, Baa, Black Sheep* (page 25)
- *Letter Cards* (page 132)
- *Baa, Baa, Black Sheep Yes and No Sort* (pages 26–27)
- *Baa, Baa, Black Sheep Rhyming Riddles* (page 28)
- *Baa, Baa, Black Sheep Reader's Theater* (pages 29–30)
- chart paper
- *Mother Goose* books or online sources

Procedures

Introducing the Rhyme

1. Copy the rhyme onto a sheet of chart paper.

2. Read the rhyme to students using a pointer to track print.

3. Ask students what they think the following words in the rhyme mean: *master*, *dame*, and *lane*. If possible, provide context clues with illustrations from Mother Goose books or online sources.

4. Distribute the *Baa, Baa, Black Sheep* rhyme (page 25) to students.

5. Read the rhyme again, and ask students to follow along on their copies. Encourage them to track print.

6. Read the rhyme chorally several times to develop fluency.

7. Allow students to illustrate the rhyme and add it to their individual poetry notebooks.

8. Have students add the title to their notebooks' tables of contents.

Change a Word

1. Distribute a set of *Letter Cards* (page 132) to each student. If this activity is used early in the year, we recommend you use only the letters they will need (*s, h, e, e, p, j, b, d, s, l*).

2. Before you begin to play, have students identify the letters and corresponding sounds.

3. Allow students time to arrange the letters to make their own words.

4. After students have had time to make and share words, ask them to put the letters in a pile and follow your instructions to make rhyming words. Say the following:

   - Let's read the rhyme together again to remind us what animal is in the rhyme. Look at the rhyme to help you make the word *sheep*. What letters did you use? (*s, h, e, e, p*)

   - Take off the first two letters. Put a new letter at the beginning to make a word that rhymes with *sheep* and means something people can ride in. What letter did you add? What word did you make? (*jeep*)

   - What word can you make that rhymes with *sheep* and *jeep* and is the sound made when you touch the jeep's horn? What letter did you change? What word did you make? (*beep*)

Baa, Baa, Black Sheep *(cont.)*

Change a Word *(cont.)*

◎ What word can you make that rhymes with *sheep, jeep,* and *beep,* and tells what you do at night in bed? What letter did you change? What word did you make? *(sleep)*

◎ Replace one letter to make the word that tells what animal is in the rhyme. What letters did you change? What word did you make? *(sheep)* What do you notice about the words we started and ended with?

Yes and No Sort ●★

1. Make a copy of the *Baa, Baa, Black Sheep Yes and No Sort* cards (pages 26–27).

2. Have students sit on the floor in a circle. Say, "We will make two piles of pictures in the middle of the circle. One will be the *yes* pile and one will be the *no* pile. Your job is to figure out why a word is a *yes* or a *no*. When you figure out the rule that makes the words *yes* or *no,* don't say it until I ask you to."

3. Hold up the *shoe* card for students to see. Tell them that the card belongs in the *yes* pile.

4. Hold up the *tie* card for students to see. Tell them that the card belongs in the *no* pile.

5. Have students sort the remaining cards into the *yes* or *no* piles.

6. Ask students for the rule (words that begin with /sh/).

Rhyming Riddles ???

1. Ask students to think of words that rhyme with the word *black.* Have them share their words with partners.

2. Record their words on the board.

3. Distribute *Baa, Baa, Black Sheep Rhyming Riddles* (page 28) to students and make connections between the words that students come up with in Step 1 to the words in the Word Bank.

4. Instruct students to use words from the Word Bank to complete the riddles.

5. Have students illustrate one of the rhyming riddles on the backs of their papers.

Writing Connection

1. As a class or in pairs, have students change the first part of *Baa, Baa, Black Sheep* by inserting other animals and their sounds or characteristics. For example:

   Moo, moo, brown cow, have you any milk? Or *Meow, meow, black cat, have you any mice?*

2. Have students share their writing with the class.

Reader's Theater

1. Distribute the *Baa, Baa, Black Sheep Reader's Theater* script (pages 29–30) to students.

2. Read the rhyme together.

3. Assign parts for five readers.

4. Allow several rehearsals to develop fluency.

5. Perform the reader's theater for the class, another class, or for a special school event.

Baa, Baa, Black Sheep

Traditional Rhyme

Baa, baa, black sheep,
have you any wool?

Yes sir, yes sir,
three bags full.

One for the
master, one
for the dame,

And one for the little boy
that lives down the lane.

Baa, Baa, Black Sheep

Yes and No Sort

Directions: Cut apart the cards. Then, sort them into two groups: a *Yes* pile and a *No* pile.

Baa, Baa, Black Sheep

Yes and No Sort *(cont.)*

Name: _____

Baa, Baa, Black Sheep
Rhyming Riddles

Directions: Use words from the Word Bank to complete the riddles about sheep.

Word Bank

pack	quack	sack	snack

1. sheep putting things in a suitcase

_____

sheep that _____

2. sheep in a bag

_____

sheep in a _____

3. sheep making sounds like a duck

_____

sheep that _____

4. sheep wanting something to eat

_____

sheep that want a _____

Baa, Baa, Black Sheep
Reader's Theater

All: Baa, Baa, Black Sheep

Reader 1: I have never seen a black sheep, only white ones.

Reader 2: I would love to see a black sheep.

Reader 3: I would love to pet a black sheep.

Reader 4: That must be where black wool comes from.

Reader 5: My dad had a black wool coat.

Reader 1: My grandma got me a wool sweater, but it made me itch.

Reader 2: What did you do with it?

Reader 1: I gave it to my brother.

Reader 3: Did it make him itch?

Baa, Baa, Black Sheep
Reader's Theater (cont.)

Reader 1: No, it did not. He liked it.

Reader 4: Maybe you are allergic to wool.

Reader 5: I am allergic to peanuts.

Reader 2: I am allergic to poison ivy.

Reader 3: I think everyone is allergic to poison ivy.

Reader 4: My grandpa can touch poison ivy and never break out with it.

Reader 5: Your grandpa is a lucky man.

Shoe Goo

Standards

- Determine or clarify the meaning of unknown and multiple-meaning words and phrases based on kindergarten reading and content.
- With prompting and support, identify the main topic and retell key details of a text.
- See Appendix C for additional standards.

Materials

- *Shoe Goo* (page 33)
- *Letter Cards* (page 132)
- *Shoe Goo Closed Word Sort* (pages 34–35)
- *Shoe Goo Rhyming Riddles* (page 36)
- *Shoe Goo Reader's Theater* (page 37)
- chart paper

Procedures

Introducing the Rhyme

1. Copy the rhyme onto a sheet of chart paper.
2. Read the rhyme to students using a pointer to track print.
3. Discuss the rhyme with students using the following questions:
   - What is happening in this poem?
   - What do you think the *goo* is? What makes you think so?
   - How do you think it got on the shoe?
   - What did the friend say to get the goo off the shoe?
   - What would you do?
   - What do you think will happen next?
4. Distribute the *Shoe Goo* rhyme (page 33) to students.
5. Read the rhyme again, and ask students to follow along on their copies. Encourage them to track print.
6. Read the rhyme chorally several times to develop fluency.
7. Allow students to illustrate the rhyme and add it to their individual poetry notebooks.
8. Have students add the title to their notebooks' tables of contents.

Change a Word

1. Distribute a set of *Letter Cards* (page 132) to each student. If this activity is used early in the year, we recommend you use only the letters they will need (*r, a, g, h, u, m, b*).
2. Before you begin the activity, have students identify the letters and corresponding sounds.
3. Allow students time to arrange the letters to make their own words.
4. After students have had time to make and share words, ask them to put the letters in a pile and follow your instructions to make a word chain from *gum* to *rag* (*gum-hum-hug-bug-rug-rag*). Say the following:
   - We will begin by making a word that is in the poem. Use three letters to make the word *gum*. What letters did you use? Let's say the word and stretch it out. (*g, u, m*)
   - Take off the letter *g*. Put a new letter at the front so that your word means making music like this (demonstrate humming). What letter did you use? What word did you make? (*hum*)
   - Take off the last letter. Put a new letter at the back so that your word means something you get along with a kiss. What letter did you use? What word did you make? (*hug*)

Shoe Goo *(cont.)*

Change a Word *(cont.)*

◎ Take off the first letter. Put a new letter at the front to make a word that describes an insect. What letter did you use? What word did you make? (*bug*)

◎ Take off the first letter. Put a new letter at the front to make another word for a small carpet. What letter did you use? What word did you make? (*rug*)

◎ We are going to end with another word that was in the poem. Take out the vowel. Put a new vowel in its place that describes what the child needs to clean his or her shoes. What letter did you use? What word did you make? (*rag*)

Closed Word Sort [color] [size] [shape]

1. Distribute sets of the *Shoe Goo Closed Word Sort* cards (pages 34–35) to individual students, pairs of students, or groups of students.

2. Ask students to put the words into two groups: words that rhyme and words that do not rhyme.

3. Follow the sorting with a discussion of the rhyming words in the poem.

Rhyming Riddles ???

1. Ask students to think of words that rhyme with *shoe* and *goo*. Have them share their words with partners.

2. Record their words on the board.

3. Distribute *Shoe Goo Rhyming Riddles* (page 36) to students and make connections between the words that students come up with in Step 1 to the words in the Word Bank.

4. Instruct students to use words from the Word Bank to complete the riddles.

5. Have students illustrate one of the rhyming riddles on the backs of their papers.

Writing Connection

1. Have students write conversations between the child in the poem and the mother when she sees the shoes.

2. Depending on the ability of the group, this can be done individually, in pairs, as dictation, or as a large group.

Reader's Theater

1. Distribute the *Shoe Goo Reader's Theater* script (page 37) to students.

2. Read the rhyme together.

3. Divide the class into three groups, and assign each group a stanza. Additionally, assign one student to be Reader 1.

4. Allow several rehearsals to develop fluency.

5. Perform the reader's theater for the class, another class, or for a special school event.

Shoe Goo

by Karen McGuigan Brothers

What's that goo
on your shoe?

Is it black
or white or blue?

White like gum
or maybe glue.

The shoes are new.
What should I do?

Wipe them with
a rag or two.

Shoe Goo

Closed Word Sort

Directions: Cut apart the cards. Then, sort them into two groups: words that rhyme and words that do not rhyme.

shoe	goo
blue	glue
gum	do
new	rag

Shoe Goo

Closed Word Sort (cont.)

two	white
what	black
is	wipe

Name: _____

Shoe Goo
Rhyming Riddles

Directions: Use words from the Word Bank to complete the riddles about shoes.

Word Bank

blue	new	grew	glue

1. shoes that you just bought

   _____

   shoes that are _____

2. shoes that are falling apart

   _____

   shoes that need _____

3. shoes the color of the sky

   _____

   shoes that are _____

4. shoes that got bigger

   _____

   shoes that _____

Shoe Goo
Reader's Theater

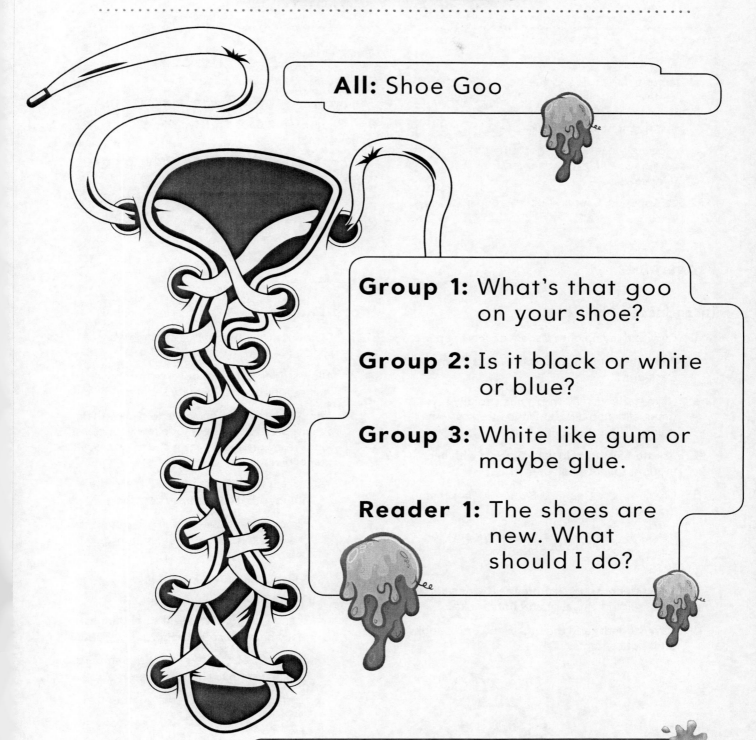

All: Shoe Goo

Group 1: What's that goo on your shoe?

Group 2: Is it black or white or blue?

Group 3: White like gum or maybe glue.

Reader 1: The shoes are new. What should I do?

All: Wipe them with a rag or two.

One, Two, Buckle My Shoe

Standards

◎ Demonstrate basic knowledge of one-to-one letter-sound correspondences by producing the primary or many of the most frequent sounds for each consonant.

◎ Associate the long and short sounds with common spellings (graphemes) for the five major vowels.

◎ See Appendix C for additional standards.

Materials

◎ *One, Two, Buckle My Shoe* (page 40)

◎ *One, Two, Buckle My Shoe Word Ladder* (page 41)

◎ *One, Two, Buckle My Shoe Open Word Sort* (pages 42–43)

◎ *One, Two, Buckle My Shoe Rhyming Riddles* (page 44)

◎ *One, Two, Buckle My Shoe Reader's Theater* (pages 45–46)

◎ chart paper

Procedures

Introducing the Rhyme

1. Copy the rhyme onto a sheet of chart paper.

2. Read the rhyme to students using a pointer to track print.

3. Have students read the rhyme chorally several times, allowing different students to use the pointer.

4. Ask students to help you come up with hand motions for each pair of lines.

5. Distribute the *One, Two, Buckle My Shoe* rhyme (page 40) to students.

6. Read the rhyme again, and ask students to follow along on their copies. Encourage them to track print.

7. Allow students to illustrate the rhyme and add it to their individual poetry notebooks.

8. Have students add the title to their notebooks' tables of contents.

Word Ladder

1. Distribute *One, Two, Buckle My Shoe Word Ladder* (page 41) to students.

2. Allow students time to observe the illustrations on their activity sheets.

3. After students have had time to review their activity sheets, tell them to follow your clues to make a word ladder from *one* to *two*. Say the following:

   ◎ start at the bottom of the ladder—the number that comes after zero (*one*)

   ◎ remove one letter—When you get up in the morning, you put your clothes _____. (*on*)

   ◎ add one letter—Some fathers have a daughter and a _____. (*son*)

   ◎ change the first letter—If something is really heavy, it could weigh a _____. (*ton*)

   ◎ change the last letter—a truck that pulls broken cars away (*tow*)

   ◎ rearrange the letters—the number that comes after one (*two*)

4. Help students make a meaningful connection between the poem and the first and last rungs of the ladder.

One, Two, Buckle My Shoe (cont.)

Open Word Sort

1. Distribute sets of the *One, Two, Buckle My Shoe Open Word Sort* cards (pages 42–43) to individual students, pairs of students, or groups of students.

2. Read the words on the cards together.

3. Have students read the words and decide how they can be sorted.

4. Follow the sorting with a discussion of word meanings and the different ways word groups were created.

Rhyming Riddles ???

1. Ask students to think of words that rhyme with the word *fat*. Have them share their words with partners.

2. Record their words on the board.

3. Distribute *One, Two, Buckle My Shoe Rhyming Riddles* (page 44) to students and make connections between the words that students come up with in Step 1 to the words in the Word Bank.

4. Instruct students to use words from the Word Bank to complete the riddles.

5. Have students illustrate one of the rhyming riddles on the backs of their papers.

Writing Connection

1. As a class or in pairs, have students change part of the rhyme using the frame below. For example: *One, Two, I love you. Three, Four, I love you more.* Or *One, Two, I need glue. Three, Four, it's in the drawer.*

   One, two, _____,

   Three, four, _____.

2. Have students share their writing with the class.

Reader's Theater

1. You can approach the *One, Two, Buckle My Shoe Reader's Theater* script (pages 45–46) in a number of ways depending on the ability of your students and the time of year. You can change the number of readers depending on the approach you use. Consider using the following:

   ◎ Write the lines on sentence strips, and pass them out to students.

   ◎ Give students scripts and have them highlight their assigned parts.

   ◎ Give the script to older reading buddies to practice and perform for the kindergartners.

2. Allow several rehearsals to develop fluency.

3. Perform the reader's theater for the class, another class, or for a special school event.

One, Two, Buckle My Shoe

Traditional Rhyme

One, two,
Buckle my shoe,

Three, four,
Shut the door,

Five, six,
Pick up sticks,

Seven, eight,
Lay them straight,

Nine, ten,
A big fat hen.

Name: _____

One, Two, Buckle My Shoe
Word Ladder

Directions: Listen to the clues. Then, write the words on the rungs below as you climb the ladder.

6. _two_

5. _____

4. _____

3. _____

2. _____

1. _one_

One, Two, Buckle My Shoe
Open Word Sort

Directions: Cut apart the cards. Then, sort them into groups that you choose. Be ready to explain your groups.

one	two
buckle	shoe
three	four
five	six
pick	sticks

One, Two, Buckle My Shoe

Open Word Sort (cont.)

seven	eight
nine	door
hen	ten
shut	lay
straight	fat

Name: _____

One, Two, Buckle My Shoe

Rhyming Riddles

Directions: Use words from the Word Bank to complete the riddles about the big fat hen.

Word Bank

bat   cat   hat   mat

1. The fat hen plays baseball. _____

The fat hen has a _____.

2. The fat hen has a new cap. _____

The fat hen has a _____.

3. The fat hen pets a kitty. _____

The fat hen pets a _____.

4. The fat hen had dirty feet. _____

The fat hen wipes them on a _____.

One, Two, Buckle My Shoe
Reader's Theater

 All: One, Two, Buckle My Shoe

 Reader 1: That's a strange rhyme.

Reader 2: Why is it strange?

 Reader 1: It doesn't tell any kind of story.

Reader 3: Maybe we could write a better one.

 Reader 4: Let me start. One, two,

 Reader 5: My puppy is new.

Reader 6: Three, four,

 Reader 7: He's from the pet store.

One, Two, Buckle My Shoe
Reader's Theater (cont.)

Reader 8: Five, six,

Reader 9: He loves to chase sticks.

Reader 10: Seven, eight,

Reader 11: He just can't wait.

Reader 12: Nine, ten,

Reader 13: To chase them again.

Reader 1: Now that tells
a real story!

The Fly

Standards

- Determine or clarify the meaning of unknown and multiple-meaning words and phrases based on kindergarten reading and content.

- Count, pronounce, blend, and segment syllables in spoken words.

- Demonstrate basic knowledge of one-to-one letter-sound correspondences by producing the primary or many of the most frequent sounds for each consonant.

- See Appendix C for additional standards.

Materials

- *The Fly* (page 49)
- *Letter Cards* (page 132)
- *The Fly Yes and No Sort* (pages 50–51)
- *The Fly Rhyming Riddles* (page 52)
- *The Fly Reader's Theater* (pages 53–54)
- chart paper

Procedures

Introducing the Rhyme

1. Copy the rhyme onto a sheet of chart paper.

2. Read the rhyme to students using a pointer to track print.

3. Discuss the rhyme with students using the following questions:
   - What is happening in this poem?
   - What did mother do to the fly? Why?
   - Why don't most people like flies?

4. Ask students to help you clap to see how many syllables are in key words from the rhyme (e.g., *fly, open, door, outside, landed, cooking, pot, mother, swat*). You might initially refer to syllables as *word parts*, but you can introduce the term *syllables* soon.

5. Distribute *The Fly* rhyme (page 49) to students.

6. Read the rhyme again, and ask students to follow along on their copies. Encourage them to track print.

7. Read the rhyme chorally several times to develop fluency.

8. Allow students to illustrate the rhyme and add it to their individual poetry notebooks.

9. Have students add the title to their notebooks' tables of contents.

Change a Word

1. Distribute a set of *Letter Cards* (page 132) to each student. If this activity is used early in the year, we recommend you use only the letters they will need (*p, p, o, t, a, n, u*).

2. Before you begin the activity, have students identify the letters and corresponding sounds.

3. Allow students time to arrange the letters to make their own words.

4. After students have had time to make and share words, ask them to put the letters in a pile and follow your instructions to make a word chain from *pot* to *pan* (*pot-top-pup-pan*). Say the following:
   - We are going to begin by making a word that is in the poem. Use three letters to make the word *pot*. What letters did you use? (*p, o, t*)
   - Now we will make a new word by starting with the last letter in *pot*. What is the last letter in *pot*? Make a word that starts with *t* that means a spinning toy. What letters did you add? What word did you make? (*top*)

The Fly (cont.)

Change a Word (cont.)

⊚ Now we will make a new word by starting with the last letter in the word *top*. What is the last letter in *top*? Make a word that starts with the letter *p* that means a baby dog. What letters did you add? What word did you make? (*pup*)

⊚ Let's do it one more time. We will make a new word by starting with the last letter in *pup*. What is the last letter in *pup*? Make a new word that is another word for *pot*. What letters did you add? What word did you make? (*pan*)

⊚ Ask students what they notice about the first and last words they made.

Yes and No Sort

1. Make a copy of *The Fly Yes and No Sort* cards (pages 50–51).

2. Have students sit on the floor in a circle. Say, "We will make two piles of pictures in the middle of the circle. One will be the *yes* pile and one will be the *no* pile. Your job is to figure out why a word is a *yes* or a *no*. When you figure out the rule that makes the words *yes* or *no*, don't say it until I ask you to."

3. Hold up the *pear* card for students to see. Tell them that the card belongs in the *yes* pile.

4. Hold up the *table* card for students to see. Tell them that the card belongs in the *no* pile.

5. Have students sort the remaining cards into the *yes* or *no* piles.

6. Ask students for the rule (words that begin with the /p/ sound).

Rhyming Riddles

1. Ask students to think of words that rhyme with the word *pot*. Have them share their words with partners.

2. Record their words on the board.

3. Distribute *The Fly Rhyming Riddles* (page 52) to students and make connections between the words that students come up with in Step 1 to the words in the Word Bank.

4. Instruct students to use words from the Word Bank to complete the riddles.

5. Have students illustrate one of the rhyming riddles on the backs of their papers.

Writing Connection

1. Have students write a list of foods that could be cooked in a pot. Encourage developmental spelling.

2. Have students share their lists with partners.

Reader's Theater

1. Distribute *The Fly Reader's Theater* script (pages 53–54) to students.

2. Read the rhyme together.

3. Assign parts for five readers.

4. Allow several rehearsals to develop fluency.

5. Perform the reader's theater for the class, another class, or for a special school event.

The Fly

by Karen McGuigan Brothers

A fly flew through
the open door;
he ate outside
but wanted more.

He landed on
the cooking pot
and mother stopped him
with a swat.

The Fly

Yes and No Sort

Directions: Cut apart the cards. Then, sort them into two groups: a *Yes* pile and a *No* pile.

The Fly
Yes and No Sort (cont.)

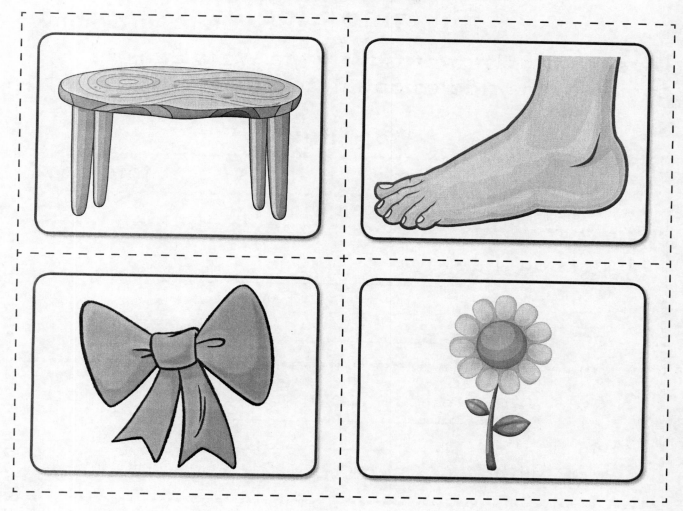

Name: _____

The Fly
Rhyming Riddles

Directions: Use words from the Word Bank to complete the riddles about pots.

Word Bank

cot	hot	knots	tots

1. pots on the stove

_____

pots that are _____

2. pots with tangled shoestrings

_____

pots with _____

3. pots that are lying down

_____

pots on a _____

4. pots that are for little children

_____

pots for _____

The Fly
Reader's Theater

All: The Fly

Reader 1: My mom hates it when a fly comes in the house.

Reader 2: Why?

Reader 1: A fly is dirty and carries germs.

Reader 3: A bee got in our house.

Reader 4: What did you do?

Reader 3: I ran, but my mom caught it in a cup and put it outside.

Reader 5: I hate bugs.

Reader 1: Some bugs are good.

Reader 2: Bees make honey for us to eat.

The Fly
Reader's Theater (cont.)

Reader 3: Butterflies are beautiful to see.

Reader 4: What about mosquitoes?

Reader 5: They are not so good.

Reader 1: Lots of things eat bugs.

Reader 2: Toads and frogs eat bugs.

Reader 3: Turtles eat bugs, too.

Reader 4: My little brother ate a bug.

Reader 5: Why did he eat a bug?

Reader 4: He did not mean to eat it. It just flew into his mouth, and he swallowed it.

Reader 2: What did he do?

Reader 4: He learned to keep his mouth closed.

To Market

Standards

- Associate the long and short sounds with common spellings (graphemes) for the five major vowels.
- Determine or clarify the meaning of unknown and multiple-meaning words and phrases based on kindergarten reading and content.
- Demonstrate basic knowledge of one-to-one letter-sound correspondences by producing the primary or many of the most frequent sounds for each consonant.
- See Appendix C for additional standards.

Materials

- *To Market* (page 57)
- *To Market Word Ladder* (page 58)
- *To Market Yes and No Sort* (pages 59–60)
- *To Market Rhyming Riddles* (page 61)
- *To Market Reader's Theater* (page 62)
- chart paper

Procedures

Introducing the Rhyme

1. Copy the rhyme onto a sheet of chart paper.
2. Read the rhyme to students using a pointer to track print.
3. Discuss the rhyme with students using the following questions:
   - Where are the people in this rhyme going?
   - What is a *market*?
   - If you bought a pig, what would you do with it?
4. Distribute the *To Market* rhyme (page 57) to students.
5. Read the rhyme again, and ask students to follow along on their copies. Encourage them to track print.
6. Read the rhyme chorally several times to develop fluency.
7. Allow students to illustrate the rhyme and add it to their individual poetry notebooks.
8. Have students add the title to their notebooks' tables of contents.

Word Ladder

1. Distribute *To Market Word Ladder* (page 58) to students.
2. Allow students time to observe the illustrations on their activity sheets.
3. After students have had time to review their activity sheets, tell them to follow your clues to make a word ladder from *fat* to *pig*. Say the following:
   - start at the bottom of the ladder—The pig was very heavy, so he was _____. (*fat*)
   - change one letter—You play baseball with a ball and a _____. (*bat*)
   - change the middle letter—I did this to my apple. (*bit*)
   - change the last letter—another word for large (*big*)
   - change the first letter—A semi-truck is sometimes called a _____. (*rig*)
   - change one letter—the animal in the rhyme (*pig*)
4. Help students make a meaningful connection between the poem and the first and last rungs of the ladder.

To Market *(cont.)*

Yes and No Sort

1. Make a copy of the *To Market Yes and No Sort* cards (pages 59–60).

2. Have students sit on the floor in a circle. Say, "We will make two piles of pictures in the middle of the circle. One will be the *yes* pile and one will be the *no* pile. Your job is to figure out why a word is a *yes* or a *no*. When you figure out the rule that makes the words *yes* or *no*, don't say it until I ask you to."

3. Hold up the *wig* card for students to see. Tell them that the card belongs in the *yes* pile.

4. Hold up the *fan* card for students to see. Tell them that the card belongs in the *no* pile.

5. Have students sort the remaining cards into the *yes* or *no* piles.

6. Ask students for the rule (words that have the short /i/ sound).

Rhyming Riddles ???

1. Have students think of words that rhyme with the word *pig*. Have them share their words with partners.

2. Record their words on the board.

3. Distribute *To Market Rhyming Riddles* (page 61) to students and make connections between the words that students come up with in Step 1 to the words in the Word Bank.

4. Instruct students to use words from the Word Bank to complete the riddles.

5. Have students illustrate one of the rhyming riddles on the backs of their papers.

Writing Connection

1. Have students write lists of items they would like to buy at the market. Encourage developmental spelling.

2. Have students share their lists with partners.

Reader's Theater

1. Distribute the *To Market Reader's Theater* script (page 62) to students.

2. Assign parts for ten readers.

3. Allow several rehearsals to develop fluency.

4. Perform the reader's theater for the class, another class, or for a special school event.

To Market

Traditional Rhyme

To market, to market,
To buy a fat pig,
Home again, home again,
Jiggedy jig.

To market, to market,
To buy a fat hog,
Home again, home again,
Jiggedy jog.

Name: _____

To Market
Word Ladder

Directions: Listen to the clues. Then, write the words on the rungs below as you climb the ladder.

6. ___pig___

5. _____

4. _____

3. _____

2. _____

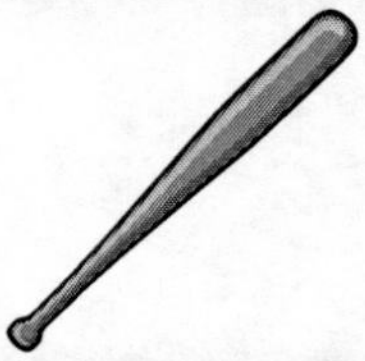

1. ___fat___

To Market

Yes and No Sort

Directions: Cut apart the cards. Then, sort them into two groups: a *Yes* pile and a *No* pile.

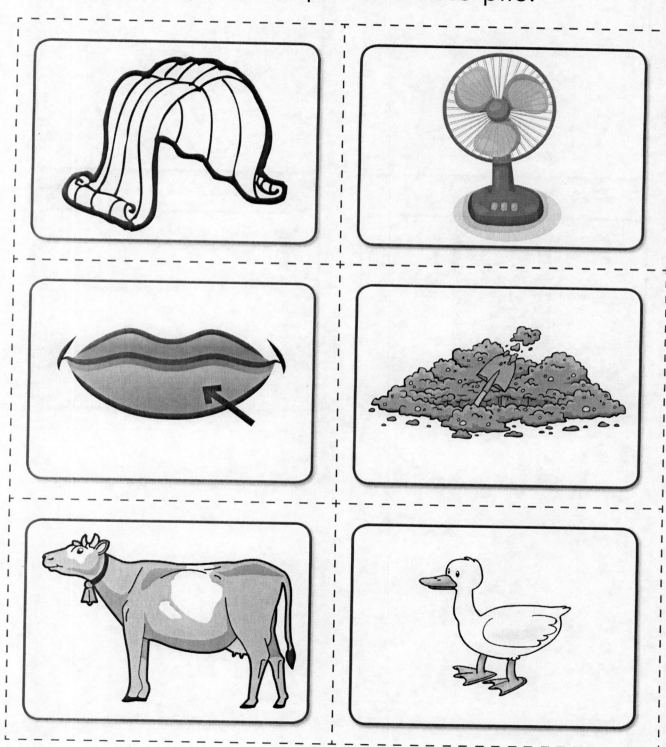

To Market

Yes and No Sort (cont.)

Name: _____

To Market

Rhyming Riddles

Directions: Use the words from the Word Bank to complete the riddles about a pig.

Word Bank

pig	wig	jig	dig

1. A pig likes shovels.

   _____

   A pig likes to _____ .

2. A pig likes to dance.

   _____

   A pig likes to _____ .

3. A pig wears things on its head.

   _____

   A pig wears a _____ .

4. A pig likes itself.

   _____

   A pig likes being a _____ .

To Market

Reader's Theater

All: To Market

Reader 1:   Why would anyone want to go to the market to buy a fat pig?

Reader 2:   I did not know you could buy a pig at a market.

Reader 3:   I think they sell pigs at the fair.

Reader 4:   I love the fair.

Reader 5:   I like to go to the fair to ride the rides.

Reader 6:   I like to go to the fair to eat the food.

Reader 7:   I like the ice cream cones.

Reader 8:   I like the hot dogs.

Reader 9:   I like the french fries.

Reader 10: I like to go to the fair to look at all the animals.

Reader 1:   Like the fat pig in our story.

Reader 2:   I am glad he found a new home.

All: Me, too!

Itsy Bitsy Spider

Standards

- ◎ Determine or clarify the meaning of unknown and multiple-meaning words and phrases based on kindergarten reading and content.
- ◎ Count, pronounce, blend, and segment syllables in spoken words.
- ◎ Isolate and pronounce the initial, medial vowel, and final sounds in three-phoneme words.
- ◎ See Appendix C for additional standards.

Materials

- ◎ *Itsy Bitsy Spider* (page 65)
- ◎ *Itsy Bitsy Spider Word Ladder* (page 66)
- ◎ *Itsy Bitsy Spider Yes and No Sort* (pages 67–68)
- ◎ *Itsy Bitsy Spider Rhyming Riddles* (page 69)
- ◎ *Itsy Bitsy Spider Reader's Theater* (pages 70–71)
- ◎ chart paper

Procedures

Introducing the Rhyme

1. Copy the rhyme onto a sheet of chart paper.
2. Read the rhyme to students using a pointer to track print.
3. Discuss the meaning of the term *water spout* (a pipe or tube for water to pass through).
4. Distribute the *Itsy Bitsy Spider* rhyme (page 65) to students.
5. Read the rhyme again, and ask students to follow along on their copies. Encourage them to track print.
6. Read the rhyme chorally several times to develop fluency.
7. Point to individual words and ask students to pat their knees and identify how many syllables they hear.
8. Allow students to illustrate the rhyme and add it to their individual poetry notebooks.
9. Have students add the title to their notebooks' tables of contents.

Word Ladder

1. Distribute *Itsy Bitsy Spider Word Ladder* (page 66) to students.
2. Allow students time to observe the illustrations on their activity sheets.
3. After students have had time to review their activity sheets, tell them to follow your clues to make a word ladder from *sun* to *rain*. Say the following:
   - ◎ start at the bottom of the ladder—a name for the object that dried up all the rain (*sun*)
   - ◎ change one letter—You put your hot dog on a _____. (*bun*)
   - ◎ change one letter—You have this when you play with your friend. (*fun*)
   - ◎ change the vowel—You use this to cool yourself off. (*fan*)
   - ◎ change the first letter—You went fast with your legs. (*ran*)
   - ◎ add one letter—What washed the spider out? (*rain*)
4. Help students make a meaningful connection between the poem and the first and last rungs of the ladder.

Itsy Bitsy Spider *(cont.)*

Yes and No Sort

1. Make a copy of the *Itsy Bitsy Spider Yes and No Sort* cards (pages 67–68).

2. Have students sit on the floor in a circle. Say, "We will make two piles of pictures in the middle of the circle. One will be the *yes* pile and one will be the *no* pile. Your job is to figure out why a word is a *yes* or a *no*. When you figure out the rule that makes the words *yes* or *no*, don't say it until I ask you to."

3. Hold up the *spider* card for students to see. Tell them that the card belongs in the *yes* pile.

4. Hold up the *pencil* card for students to see. Tell them that the card belongs in the *no* pile.

5. Have students sort the remaining cards into the *yes* or *no* piles.

6. Ask students for the rule (words that begin with the /s/ sound).

Rhyming Riddles

1. Ask students to think of words that rhyme with the word *sun*. Have them share their words with partners.

2. Record their words on the board.

3. Distribute *Itsy Bitsy Spider Rhyming Riddles* (page 69) to students and make connections between the words that students come up with in Step 1 to the words in the Word Bank.

4. Instruct students to use words from the Word Bank to complete the riddles.

5. Have students illustrate one of the rhyming riddles on the backs of their papers.

Writing Connection

1. Have students list as many words as they can that begin with the letter *s*. Encourage developmental spelling.

2. Have students share their lists and keep track of how many words were listed.

Reader's Theater 🎭

1. Distribute the *Itsy Bitsy Spider Reader's Theater* script (pages 70–71) to students.

2. Assign parts for five readers.

3. Allow several rehearsals to develop fluency.

4. Perform the reader's theater for the class, another class, or for a special school event.

Itsy Bitsy Spider

Traditional Rhyme

The Itsy Bitsy spider
Climbed up the water spout;

Down came the rain
And washed the spider out.

Out came the sun
And dried up all the rain;

And the Itsy Bitsy spider
Climbed up the spout again.

Name: _____

Itsy Bitsy Spider
Word Ladder

....

Directions: Listen to the clues. Then, write the words on the rungs below as you climb the ladder.

6. ___ rain ___

5. _____

4. _____

3. _____

2. _____

1. ___ sun ___

Itsy Bitsy Spider

Yes and No Sort

Directions: Cut apart the cards. Then, sort them into two groups: a *Yes* pile and a *No* pile.

Itsy Bitsy Spider

Yes and No Sort (cont.)

Name: _____

Itsy Bitsy Spider

Rhyming Riddles

Directions: Use words from the Word Bank to complete the riddles about the spider.

Word Bank

sun	run	fun	bun

1. a spider with a tan

    _____

    a spider that was in the _____

2. a spider playing at the park

    _____

    a spider having _____

3. a spider eating a hot dog

    _____

    a spider eating a _____

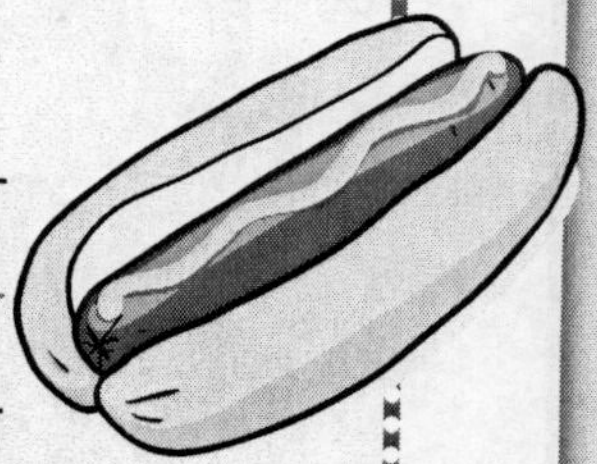

4. a spider going fast

    _____

    a spider that can _____

Itsy Bitsy Spider
Reader's Theater

 All: Itsy Bitsy Spider

 Reader 1: If the spider got washed out, why did he climb the spout again?

Reader 2: Maybe it was fun.

 Reader 3: Why would it be fun?

 Reader 2: When the rain came, it was like a big water slide.

 Reader 4: I like water slides.

 Reader 5: We went to a water slide last summer.

 Reader 1: We have a pool.

 Reader 2: I like to swim in the lake.

 Reader 3: Do fish ever come up and try to bite you?

Itsy Bitsy Spider

Reader's Theater *(cont.)*

Reader 2: No. The fish swim away.

Reader 4: Fish don't bite.

Reader 5: What about sharks?
They bite.

Reader 1: There are no sharks in a lake.

Reader 2: Sometimes there are water
slides at a lake.

Reader 3: I tried to go down a slide in
my wet bathing suit, but I
got stuck.

Reader 4: Why did you get stuck?

Reader 3: Because the slide was dry
and I was wet.

Reader 5: That would not happen in
the rain.

Reader 1: You would slide right down
just like the spider did.

Hark! Hark!

Standards

- Form regular, plural nouns orally by adding /s/ or /es/.
- Determine or clarify the meaning of unknown and multiple-meaning words and phrases based on kindergarten reading and content.
- See Appendix C for additional standards.

Materials

- *Hark! Hark!* (page 74)
- *Hark! Hark! Word Ladder* (page 75)
- *Hark! Hark! Closed Word Sort* (pages 76–77)
- *Hark! Hark! Rhyming Riddles* (page 78)
- *Hark! Hark! Reader's Theater* (pages 79–80)
- chart paper

Procedures

Introducing the Rhyme

1. Copy the rhyme onto a sheet of chart paper.

2. Read the rhyme to students using a pointer to track print.

3. Discuss the rhyme with students using the following questions:
   - What do you think the word *hark* means?
   - What is happening in this poem?
   - Why are the dogs barking?
   - What are *beggars*?
   - What is a velvet gown?

4. Distribute the *Hark! Hark!* rhyme (page 74) to students.

5. Read the rhyme again, and ask students to follow along on their copies.

6. Allow students to illustrate the rhyme and add it to their individual poetry notebooks.

7. Have students add the title to their notebooks' tables of contents.

Word Ladder

1. Distribute *Hark! Hark! Word Ladder* (page 75) to students.

2. Allow students time to observe the illustrations on their activity sheets.

3. After students have had time to review their activity sheets, tell them to follow your clues to make a word ladder from *man* to *tags*. Say the following:
   - start at the bottom of the ladder—A grown boy is a _____. (*man*)
   - change the first letter—You use this to cool yourself off. (*fan*)
   - change the first letter—You went fast with your legs. (*ran*)
   - change the first letter—You got this in the sun. (*tan*)
   - change the last letter—This tells you how much clothes cost. (*tag*)
   - add one letter—More than one tag makes the word _____. (*tags*)

4. Help students make a meaningful connection between the poem and the first and last rungs of the ladder.

Hark! Hark! *(cont.)*

Closed Word Sort

1. Distribute sets of the *Hark! Hark! Closed Word Sort* cards (pages 76–77) to individual students, pairs of students, or groups of students.

2. Read the words on the cards together.

3. Have students sort their cards into piles based on words that rhyme.

4. Relate the words to the rhyme.

Rhyming Riddles ???

1. Ask students to think of words that rhyme with the word *hark*. Have them share their words with partners.

2. Record their words on the board.

3. Distribute *Hark! Hark! Rhyming Riddles* (page 78) to students and make connections between the words that students come up with in Step 1 to the words in the Word Bank.

4. Instruct students to use words from the Word Bank to complete the riddles.

5. Have students illustrate one of the rhyming riddles on the backs of their papers.

Writing Connection

1. Model for students how to fold a sheet of paper vertically to create two columns.

2. Have students label the first column *dogs*. Have them label the second column *bark*.

3. Have students list as many animals and their corresponding sounds as they can think of (e.g., *cow/moo; cat/meow*). Encourage developmental spelling.

4. Have students share their lists with the class.

5. Keep track of how many different animal/sound pairs were listed.

Reader's Theater

1. Distribute the *Hark! Hark! Reader's Theater* script (pages 79–80) to students.

2. Assign parts for five readers.

3. Allow several rehearsals to develop fluency.

4. Perform the reader's theater for the class, another class, or for a special school event.

Hark! Hark!

Traditional Rhyme

Hark, hark,

The dogs do bark,

Beggars are coming to town:

Some in rags,

Some in tags,

And some in velvet gowns.

Name: _____

Hark! Hark!
Word Ladder

Directions: Listen to the clues. Then, write the words on the rungs below as you climb the ladder.

6. _tags_

5. _____

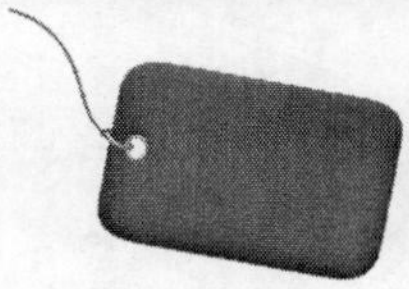

4. _____

3. _____

2. _____

1. _man_

Hark! Hark!

Closed Word Sort

Directions: Cut apart the cards. Then, sort them into groups of words that rhyme.

rags	tags
bags	sags
wags	dogs
jogs	logs

Hark! Hark!

Closed Word Sort (cont.)

hogs	bark
dark	mark
park	bogs

Name: _____

Hark! Hark!

Rhyming Riddles

· ·

Directions: Use words from the Word Bank to complete the riddles about dogs.

Word Bank

park   dark   bark   mark

1. dogs making noise

_____

dogs that _____

2. dogs at night

_____

dogs in the _____

3. dogs at a playground

_____

dogs at a _____

4. dogs that draw lines on things

_____

dogs that _____

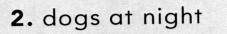

Hark! Hark!
Reader's Theater

All: Hark! Hark!

Reader 1: I wonder what *hark* means.

Reader 2: I think it means listen.

Reader 3: It must mean listen to the dogs bark.

Reader 4: Why were the dogs barking?

Reader 5: Because the beggars were coming.

Reader 1: What's a beggar?

Reader 2: I think it is someone who begs for food.

Reader 3: Maybe it is someone who begs for money.

Reader 4: I think the story is about Halloween.

Hark! Hark!
Reader's Theater (cont.)

Reader 5: Why do you think that?

Reader 4: Because at Halloween, we have Beggar's Night.

Reader 1: That is where everyone dresses in costume and goes from door to door begging for candy.

Reader 2: That is why some beggars in the story were dressed in rags, some in tags, and some in velvet gowns.

All: That sounds like Halloween to me!

Diddle, Diddle, Dumpling

Standards

- Determine or clarify the meaning of unknown and multiple-meaning words and phrases based on kindergarten reading and content.
- Understand and use question words (interrogatives) (e.g., who, what, where, when, why, how).
- See Appendix C for additional standards.

Materials

- *Diddle, Diddle, Dumpling* (page 83)
- *Letter Cards* (page 132)
- *Diddle, Diddle, Dumpling Open Word Sort* (pages 84–85)
- *Diddle, Diddle, Dumpling Rhyming Riddles* (page 86)
- *Diddle, Diddle, Dumpling Reader's Theater* (pages 87–88)
- chart paper

Procedures

Introducing the Rhyme

1. Copy the rhyme onto a sheet of chart paper.
2. Read the rhyme to students using a pointer to track print.
3. Discuss the rhyme with students using the following questions:
   - Who is telling about John? How do you know?
   - What are *stockings*?
   - What did John do?
   - Why do you think he did that?
4. Distribute the *Diddle, Diddle, Dumpling* rhyme (page 83) to students.
5. Read the rhyme again, and ask students to follow along on their copies.
6. Allow students to illustrate the rhyme and add it to their individual poetry notebooks.
7. Have students add the title to their notebooks' tables of contents.

Change a Word

1. Distribute a set of *Letter Cards* (page 132) to each student. If this activity is used early in the year, we recommend you use only the letters they will need (*s, o, c, k, s, r, l, b, c, d*).
2. Before you begin the activity, have students identify the letters and corresponding sounds.
3. Allow students time to arrange the letters to make their own words.
4. After students have had time to make and share words, ask them to put the letters in a pile and follow your instructions. Say the following:
   - John went to bed with stockings on. What is another word for stocking? (Help students encode the word *socks* by stretching out the sounds.)
   - Change the beginning letter so that you have a word that means the same thing as stones. What letter did you use? What word did you make? (*rocks*)
   - Change the beginning letter so that you have a word that tells what keys open. What letters did you use? What word did you make? (*locks*)
   - Add a letter at the beginning to make a word that describes a wooden toy you build with. What letter did you add? What word did you make? (*blocks*)

Diddle, Diddle, Dumpling (cont.)

Change a Word (cont.)

- ◎ Change the first letter to make a word for something you use to tell time. What letter did you use? What word did you make? (*clocks*)

- ◎ Change the beginning of the word *clocks* to describe a place where boats park. How did you change the beginning? What word did you make? (*docks*)

- ◎ Change the beginning letter to tell what John had on when he went to bed. What letter did you use? What word did you make? (*socks*)

- ◎ Ask students what they notice about the first and last words they made.

Open Word Sort color size shape

1. Distribute sets of the *Diddle, Diddle, Dumpling Open Word Sort* cards (pages 84–85) to individuals, pairs, or groups of students.

2. Read the words on the cards together.

3. Have students sort their cards to create matches based on what the words have in common. Provide support with word recognition as needed.

4. Follow with a discussion of word pairs.

5. Ask students to identify words that are related to the rhyme.

Rhyming Riddles ???

1. Ask students to think of words that rhyme with the word *son*. Have them share their words with partners.

2. Record their words on the board.

3. Distribute *Diddle, Diddle, Dumpling Rhyming Riddles* (page 86) to students. Make connections between the words created from Step 1 and the words in the Word Bank.

4. Instruct students to use words from the Word Bank to complete the riddles.

5. Have students illustrate one of the rhyming riddles on the backs of their papers.

Writing Connection

1. As a class, in groups, or in pairs, have students write a copy change of the first part of the rhyme by inserting their own names. Copy change is a writing activity where the writer borrows the structure of another text and uses it as a skeleton for his or her own piece.

> **Examples**
>
> Diddle, Diddle, Dumpling
>
> My daughter Lily,
>
> She went to bed
>
> And acted silly.
>
>
> Diddle, Diddle, Dumpling,
>
> My son Jack,
>
> He went to bed
>
> After he ate a snack.

2. Have students share their writing with the class.

Reader's Theater

1. Distribute the *Diddle, Diddle, Dumpling Reader's Theater* script (pages 87–88) to students.

2. Assign parts for five readers.

3. Allow several rehearsals to develop fluency.

4. Perform the reader's theater for the class, another class, or for a special school event.

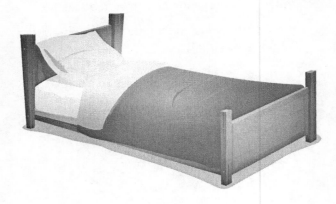

Diddle, Diddle, Dumpling

Traditional Rhyme

Diddle, diddle, dumpling,
my son John

Went to bed with his
stockings on.

One shoe off, and one
shoe on.

Diddle, diddle, dumpling,
my son John

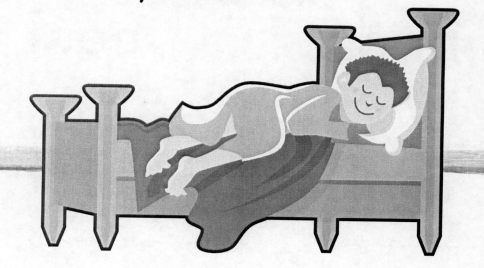

Diddle, Diddle, Dumpling
Open Word Sort

Directions: Cut apart the cards. Then, sort them into matches based on what the words have in common.

shoe	sock
monkey	banana
hand	mitten
bird	nest
bat	ball

 #51336—Rhythm & Rhyme Literacy Time

Diddle, Diddle, Dumpling
Open Word Sort (cont.)

teeth	toothbrush
mouse	cheese
lock	key
sun	sunglasses

Name: _____

Diddle, Diddle, Dumpling

Rhyming Riddles

Directions: Use words from the Word Bank to complete the riddles about John.

Word Bank

run	bun	done	won

1. My son John ate a hot dog.

_____

_ _ _ _ _ _ _ _ _

My son ate a hot dog on a _____.

2. My son John was the winner of the game.

_____

_ _ _ _ _ _ _ _ _

My son _____.

3. My son John goes fast with his legs.

_____

_ _ _ _ _ _ _ _ _

My son can _____.

4. My son John finished his lunch.

_____

_ _ _ _ _ _ _ _ _

My son is _____.

Diddle, Diddle, Dumpling
Reader's Theater

All: Diddle, Diddle, Dumpling

Reader 1: John must have been very tired.

Reader 2: That is why he went to bed with his clothes on.

Reader 3: My mother makes me change into my pajamas before I go to bed.

Reader 4: My mother makes us go to bed before we get that tired.

Reader 5: I always take a bath before I go to bed. It makes me sleepy.

Reader 1: In the winter, I like to sleep under lots of blankets.

Reader 2: I like to wear socks to bed in the winter to keep my feet warm.

Reader 1: It gets dark very early in the winter.

Diddle, Diddle, Dumpling

Reader's Theater *(cont.)*

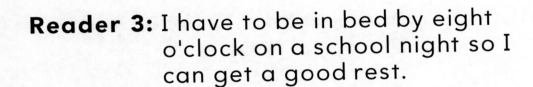

Reader 3: I have to be in bed by eight o'clock on a school night so I can get a good rest.

Reader 4: My mom lets me stay up until nine o'clock on the weekends.

Reader 5: I like to go camping and sleep in a tent.

Reader 4: My mom lets me sleep in a sleeping bag on the floor sometimes.

Reader 2: When I have a sleepover, we always sleep on the floor.

Reader 3: I like to sleep because I like to dream.

Reader 1: When it comes to sleeping, I like my bed the best.

My Dog Joe

Standards

- Isolate and pronounce the initial, medial vowel, and final sounds in three-phoneme words.
- Add or substitute individual sounds (phonemes) in simple, one-syllable words to make new words.
- With guidance and support from adults, respond to questions and suggestions from peers and add details to strengthen writing as needed.
- See Appendix C for additional standards.

Materials

- *My Dog Joe* (page 91)
- *My Dog Joe Word Ladder* (page 92)
- *My Dog Joe Closed Word Sort* (pages 93–94)
- *My Dog Joe Rhyming Riddles* (page 95)
- *My Dog Joe Reader's Theater* (pages 96–97)
- chart paper

Procedures

Introducing the Rhyme

1. Copy the rhyme onto a sheet of chart paper.
2. Read the rhyme to students using a pointer to track print.
3. Point out each verse and introduce the word *stanza* to children.
4. Distribute the *My Dog Joe* rhyme (page 91) to students.
5. Have children read the rhyme chorally from their copies to develop fluency.
6. Allow students to illustrate the rhyme and add it to their individual poetry notebooks.
7. Have students add the title to their notebooks' tables of contents.

Word Ladder

1. Distribute *My Dog Joe Word Ladder* (page 92) to students.
2. Allow students time to observe the illustrations on their activity sheets.
3. After students have had time to review their activity sheets, tell them to follow your clues to make a word ladder from *dog* to *pal*. Say the following:
   - start at the bottom of the ladder—the animal in the rhyme (*dog*)
   - change the last letter—the mark that goes over the letter *i* (*dot*)
   - change the first letter—a word to describe fire (*hot*)
   - change the vowel—something you wear on your head (*hat*)
   - change the first letter—a soft touch (*pat*)
   - change the last letter—another word for friend (*pal*)
4. Help students make a meaningful connection between the poem and the first and last rungs of the ladder.

My Dog Joe *(cont.)*

Closed Word Sort `color` `size` `shape`

1. Distribute sets of the *My Dog Joe Closed Word Sort* cards (pages 93–94) to individual students, pairs of students, or groups of students.

2. Read the words on the cards together.

3. Have students sort their cards into two groups: words that name living things and words that name nonliving things. Provide support with word recognition as needed.

4. Follow the sorting with a discussion of the words.

5. Discuss words related to the rhyme.

Rhyming Riddles

1. Ask students to think of words that rhyme with the word *dog*. Have them share their words with partners.

2. Record their words on the board.

3. Distribute *My Dog Joe Rhyming Riddles* (page 95) to students and make connections between the words that students come up with in Step 1 to the words in the Word Bank.

4. Instruct students to use words from the Word Bank to complete the riddles.

5. Have students illustrate one of the rhyming riddles on the backs of their papers.

Writing Connection

1. As a class, in groups, or in pairs, have students write a copy change using the following pattern:

> **Examples**
>
> I have a dog,
>
> His name is Fred;
>
> He's not allowed
>
> Upon the bed.
>
> I have a dog,
>
> Her name is Jenny;
>
> I hope she didn't
>
> Swallow my penny.
>
> I have a dog,
>
> Her name is Tad
>
> Sometimes she's good
>
> and sometimes she's bad.

2. Have students share their writing with the class.

Reader's Theater

1. Distribute the *My Dog Joe Reader's Theater* script (pages 96–97) to students.

2. Assign parts for five readers.

3. Allow several rehearsals to develop fluency.

4. Perform the reader's theater for the class, another class, or for a special school event.

My Dog Joe

By Karen McGuigan Brothers

I have a dog,
His name is Joe;
He follows me
Wherever I go.

He's not too fat
And not too tall;
He likes to play
And catch his ball.

He likes to sleep
With me in bed;
I hug his neck
And pat his head.

I love my dog
And tell him so;
He's my best friend,
My pal, my Joe.

Name: _____

My Dog Joe
Word Ladder

Directions: Listen to the clues. Then, write the words on the rungs below as you climb the ladder.

6. pal

5. _____

4. _____

3. _____

2. _____

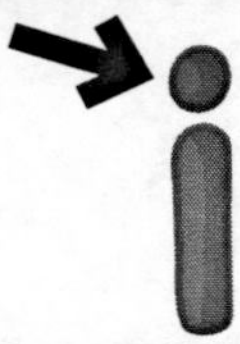

1. dog

My Dog Joe
Closed Word Sort

Directions: Cut apart the cards. Then, sort them into two groups: words that name living things and words that name nonliving things.

hog	pig
gum	dog
cat	wig
pan	pot
mop	lip

My Dog Joe
Closed Word Sort (cont.)

hen	bug
mom	bat
man	bag
hat	rat

Name: _____

My Dog Joe

Rhyming Riddles

Directions: Use words from the Word Bank to complete the riddles about a dog.

Word Bank

log	fog	hog	jog

1. My dog likes to run on the track.

_____

My dog likes to _____.

2. My dog sits on a tree branch.

_____

My dog sits on a _____.

3. My dog sees a very large pig.

_____

My dog sees a _____.

4. There is a cloud over my dog.

_____

My dog is in the _____.

My Dog Joe
Reader's Theater

All: My Dog Joe

Reader 1: I like dogs.

Reader 2: I have a dog.

Reader 3: Does he sleep with you in bed?

Reader 2: Yes. He sleeps right beside me.

Reader 4: My dog likes to chase cats, but he never catches them.

Reader 5: My dog has a box full of toys. He likes the ones that make noise when he bites them.

Reader 1: My dog does not like to get a bath. He tries to hide.

Reader 2: My dog likes to take walks with me.

Reader 3: When my dog is good, I give her a dog cookie.

My Dog Joe
Reader's Theater *(cont.)*

Reader 4: My dog likes to take rides in the car with his head sticking out the window.

Reader 5: I think dogs are almost like people because they are so smart.

Reader 1: My mom says that our dog is like part of our family.

All: I love dogs.

Molly, Molly

Standards

- Determine or clarify the meaning of unknown and multiple-meaning words and phrases based on kindergarten reading and content.
- Count, pronounce, blend, and segment syllables in spoken words.
- Isolate and pronounce the initial, medial vowel, and final sounds in three-phoneme words.
- See Appendix C for additional standards.

Materials

- *Molly, Molly* (page 100)
- *Molly, Molly Word Ladder* (page 101)
- *Molly, Molly Open Word Sort* (page 102)
- *Molly, Molly Rhyming Riddles* (page 103)
- *Molly, Molly Reader's Theater* (pages 104–105)
- chart paper

Procedures

Introducing the Rhyme

1. Copy the rhyme onto a sheet of chart paper.

2. Read the rhyme to students using a pointer to track print.

3. Discuss the rhyme with students using the following questions:
   - What was Molly's present?
   - Who was her present from?
   - What happened to her present?
   - Where do you think it was?
   - What do you think Molly will do next?

4. Record students' responses on the sheet of chart paper.

5. Point to individual words in the rhyme, and ask students to pat their knees in order to identify how many syllables are in the words.

6. Distribute the *Molly, Molly* rhyme (page 100) to students.

7. Read the rhyme again, and ask students to follow along on their copies.

8. Allow students to illustrate the rhyme and add it to their individual poetry notebooks.

9. Have students add the title to their notebooks' tables of contents.

Word Ladder

1. Distribute *Molly, Molly Word Ladder* (page 101) to students.

2. Allow students time to observe the illustrations on their activity sheets.

3. After students have had time to review their activity sheets, tell them to follow your clues to make a word ladder from *sad* to *glad*. Say the following:
   - start at the bottom of the ladder—how Molly felt when she lost her dolly (*sad*)
   - change the last letter—You put yourself in a chair. (*sat*)
   - change the first letter—what you use to hit a ball (*bat*)
   - change the first letter—You wipe your muddy boots on this. (*mat*)
   - change the last letter—another word for angry (*mad*)
   - change the beginning sound—how Molly felt when she found her doll (*glad*)

4. Help students make a meaningful connection between the poem and the first and last rungs of the ladder.

Molly, Molly *(cont.)*

Open Word Sort color size shape

1. Distribute sets of the *Molly, Molly Open Word Sort* cards (page 102) to individual students, pairs of students, or groups of students.

2. Read the words on the cards together.

3. Have students read the words and decide how they can be sorted.

4. Follow the sorting with a discussion of word meanings and the different ways word groups were created.

5. Discuss the words that are related to the rhyme.

Rhyming Riddles ???

1. Ask students to think of words that rhyme with the word *doll*. Have them share their words with partners.

2. Record their words on the board.

3. Distribute *Molly, Molly Rhyming Riddles* (page 103) to students and make connections between the words that students come up with in Step 1 to the words in the Word Bank.

4. Instruct students to use words from the Word Bank to complete the riddles.

5. Have students illustrate one of the rhyming riddles on the backs of their papers.

Writing Connection

1. Have students write lists of all the places Molly could have lost her doll. Encourage developmental spelling.

2. Have students share their lists with partners.

Reader's Theater

1. Distribute the *Molly, Molly Reader's Theater* script (pages 104–105) to students.

2. Assign parts for six readers.

3. Allow several rehearsals to develop fluency.

4. Perform the reader's theater for the class, another class, or for a special school event.

Molly, Molly

By Karen McGuigan Brothers

Molly, Molly
Got a dolly
A present from her dad.

Molly, Molly
Named her Polly,
The only doll she had.

Molly, Molly
Lost her dolly,
It made her very sad.

Molly, Molly
Found her dolly
And now she's oh so glad.

Name: _____

Molly, Molly
Word Ladder

Directions: Listen to the clues. Then, write the words on the rungs below as you climb the ladder.

6. glad

5.

4.

3.

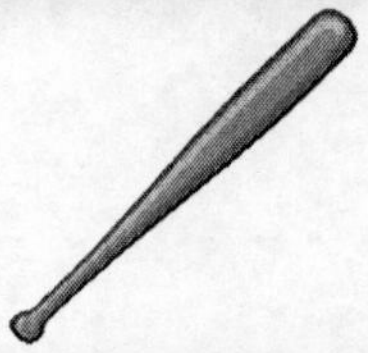

2.

1. sad

Molly, Molly
Open Word Sort

Directions: Cut apart the cards. Then, sort them into groups that you choose. Be ready to explain your groups.

dolly	doll
dad	gift
Molly	Polly
sad	found
glad	father

#51336—*Rhythm & Rhyme Literacy Time* © Shell Education

Name: _____

Molly, Molly
Rhyming Riddles

Directions: Use words from the Word Bank to complete the riddles about a doll.

Word Bank

call   tall   fall   wall

1. Molly's doll has a phone.

_____

Molly's doll can _____ a friend.

2. Molly's doll is not short.

_____

Molly's doll is _____.

3. Molly's doll is sitting by Humpty Dumpty.

_____

Molly's doll is sitting on a _____.

4. Molly's doll is hurt.

_____

Molly's doll had a bad _____.

Molly, Molly
Reader's Theater

All: Molly, Molly

Reader 1: I feel bad for Molly.

Reader 2: Why?

Reader 1: She only had one dolly.

Reader 3: It was a present.

Reader 4: I like presents.

Reader 5: I like to open them.

Reader 6: I like to get toys.

Reader 1: I like to get games.

Reader 2: My best present was a puppy.

Reader 3: I know what I would not like to find in a present.

Reader 4: What?

Molly, Molly
Reader's Theater (cont.)

Reader 3: Clothes.

Reader 4: My grandma gets me clothes.

Reader 5: What do you say?

Reader 4: I say, "Thank you." I would not want to hurt her feelings.

Reader 1: Yes. It is not nice to hurt your grandma's feelings.

Reader 6: It's not nice to hurt anyone's feelings.

Handy-Spandy, Jack-A-Dandy

Standards

- Determine or clarify the meaning of unknown and multiple-meaning words and phrases based on kindergarten reading and content.

- Add or substitute individual sounds (phonemes) in simple, one-syllable words to make new words.

- See Appendix C for additional standards.

Materials

- *Handy-Spandy, Jack-A-Dandy* (page 108)

- *Letter Cards* (page 132)

- *Handy-Spandy, Jack-A-Dandy Yes and No Sort* (pages 109–110)

- *Handy-Spandy, Jack-A-Dandy Rhyming Riddles* (page 111)

- *Handy-Spandy, Jack-A-Dandy Reader's Theater* (page 112)

- chart paper

Procedures

Introducing the Rhyme 🎤

1. Copy the rhyme onto a sheet of chart paper.

2. Ask students what they think the following words mean: *dandy*, *plum*, *grocer*, and *handy*. Provide context clues as needed.

3. Distribute the *Handy-Spandy, Jack-A-Dandy* rhyme (page 108) to students.

4. Read the rhyme, and ask students to follow along on their copies. Encourage them to track print.

5. Allow students to illustrate the rhyme and add it to their individual poetry notebooks.

6. Have students add the title to their notebooks' tables of contents.

Change a Word (abc)

1. Distribute a set of *Letter Cards* (page 132) to each student. If this activity is used early in the year, we recommend you use only the letters they will need (s, h, o, p, p, t, m, h).

2. Before you begin the activity, have students identify the letters and corresponding sounds.

3. Allow students time to arrange the letters to make their own words.

4. After students have had time to make and share words, ask them to put the letters in a pile and follow your instructions. Say the following:

- Let's read the rhyme together again to remind us where Jack-A-Dandy went. Make the word that tells where he went. What letters did you use? What word did you make? (*shop*)

- Take off the first two letters. Put a new letter at the beginning to make a word that rhymes with *shop* and means soda. It's also a word some children use for their father or grandfather. What letter did you add? What word did you make? (*pop*)

- What word can you make that rhymes with *shop* and *pop* and is the word for a spinning toy? What letter did you change? What word did you make? (*top*)

- What word can you make that rhymes with *shop*, *pop*, and *top* and is the word for something you use to clean the floor? What letter did you change? What word did you make? (*mop*)

- What word can you make that rhymes with *shop*, *pop*, *top*, and *mop* and is the word that tells how Jack-A-Dandy went home? What letter did you change? What word did you make? (*hop*)

Handy-Spandy, Jack-A-Dandy *(cont.)*

Yes and No Sort

1. Make a copy of the *Handy-Spandy, Jack-A-Dandy Yes and No Sort* cards (pages 109–110).

2. Have students sit on the floor in a circle. Say, "We will make two piles of pictures in the middle of the circle. One will be the *yes* pile and one will be the *no* pile. Your job is to figure out why a word is a *yes* or a *no*. When you figure out the rule that makes the words *yes* or *no*, don't say it until I ask you to."

3. Hold up the *cheese* card for students to see. Tell them that the card belongs in the *yes* pile.

4. Hold up the *hat* card for students to see. Tell them that the card belongs in the *no* pile.

5. Have students sort the remaining cards into the *yes* or *no* piles.

6. Ask students for the rule (food).

Rhyming Riddles ???

1. Have students think of words that rhyme with the word *Jack.* Have them share their words with partners.

2. Record their words on the board.

3. Distribute *Handy-Spandy, Jack-A-Dandy Rhyming Riddles* (page 111) to students and make connections between the words that students come up with in Step 1 to the words in the Word Bank.

4. Instruct students to use the words from the Word Bank to complete the riddles.

5. Have students illustrate one of the rhyming riddles on the backs of their papers.

Writing Connection 📝

1. Discuss the rule for capitalization of the word *I*.

2. Discuss with students how to correctly use the period and the exclamation point at the end of a sentence.

3. Have students make lists of things they love. Write the following sentence frame to help students successfully complete their sentence: *I love _____.* or *I love _____!* Encourage developmental spelling.

4. Have students share their lists with partners.

Reader's Theater 🎭

1. Distribute the *Handy-Spandy, Jack-A-Dandy Reader's Theater* script (page 112) to students.

2. Assign parts for five readers.

3. Allow several rehearsals to develop fluency.

4. Perform the reader's theater for the class, another class, or for a special school event.

Handy-Spandy, Jack-A-Dandy

Traditional Rhyme

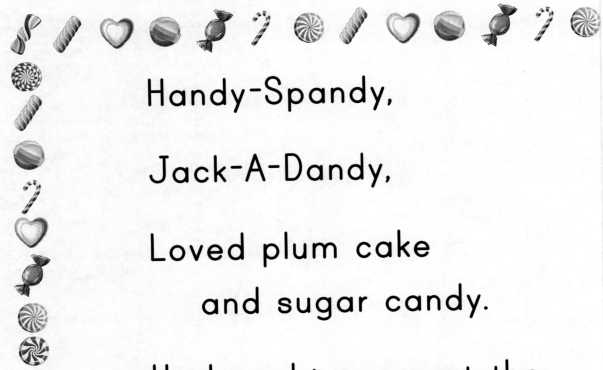

Handy-Spandy,

Jack-A-Dandy,

Loved plum cake
and sugar candy.

He bought some at the
grocer's shop,

And out he came,
hop, hop, hop.

Handy-Spandy, Jack-A-Dandy

Yes and No Sort

Directions: Cut apart the cards. Then, sort them into two groups: a *Yes* pile and a *No* pile.

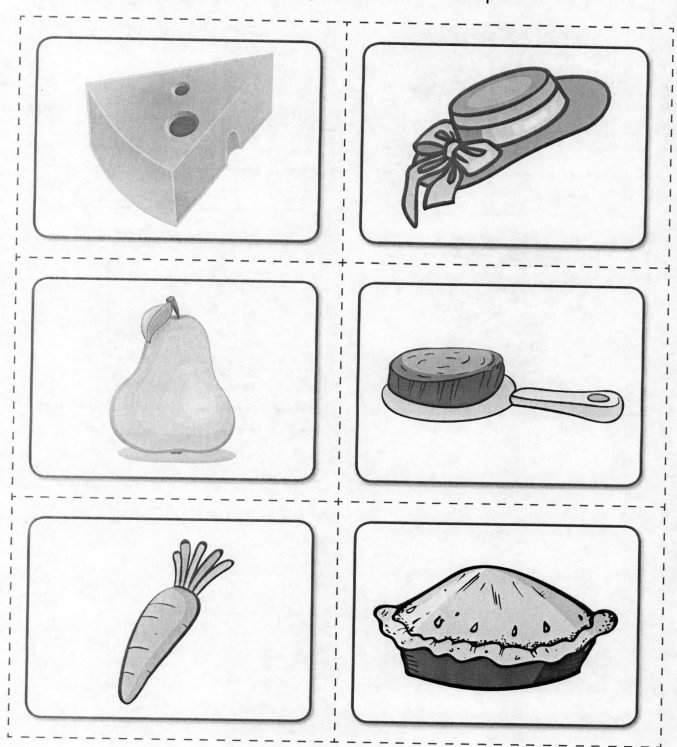

Handy-Spandy, Jack-A-Dandy
Yes and No Sort *(cont.)*

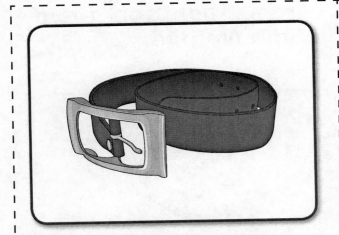

Name: _____

Handy-Spandy, Jack-A-Dandy
Rhyming Riddles

Directions: Use words from the Word Bank to complete the riddles about Jack.

Word Bank

| black | back | pack | quack |

1. Jack likes his suitcase.

_____

Jack likes to _____ .

2. Jack does not like the front.

_____

Jack likes the _____ .

3. Jack likes dark colors.

_____

Jack likes _____ .

4. Jack likes to sound like a duck.

_____

Jack likes to _____ .

Handy-Spandy, Jack-A-Dandy
Reader's Theater

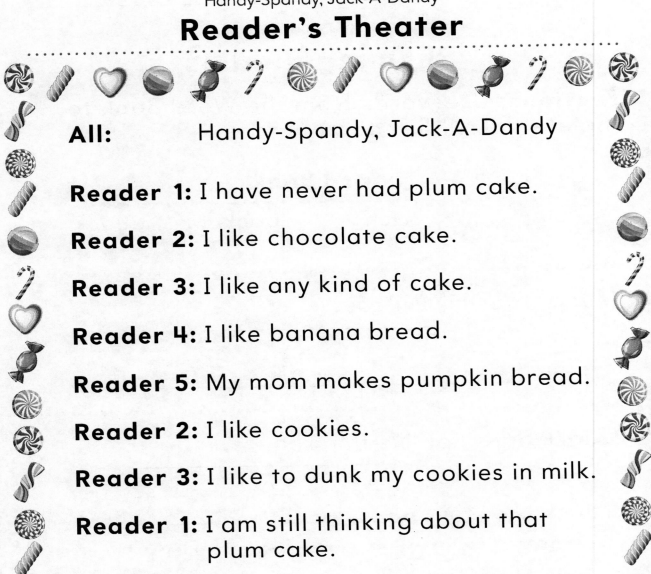

All: Handy-Spandy, Jack-A-Dandy

Reader 1: I have never had plum cake.

Reader 2: I like chocolate cake.

Reader 3: I like any kind of cake.

Reader 4: I like banana bread.

Reader 5: My mom makes pumpkin bread.

Reader 2: I like cookies.

Reader 3: I like to dunk my cookies in milk.

Reader 1: I am still thinking about that plum cake.

Reader 2: I am going to ask my mom to bake one.

Reader 3: Jack-A-Dandy loved it.

Reader 4: I wonder what it would taste like.

Reader 5: Not as good as the sugar candy he bought!

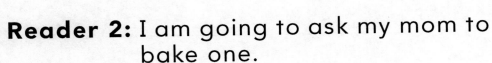

Pat-A-Cake, Pat-A-Cake, Baker's Man

Standards

◎ Isolate and pronounce the initial, medial vowel, and final sounds (phonemes) in three-phoneme words.

◎ Add or substitute individual sounds (phonemes) in simple, one-syllable words to make new words.

◎ Demonstrate basic knowledge of one-to-one letter-sound correspondences by producing the primary or many of the most frequent sounds for each consonant.

◎ See Appendix C for additional standards.

Materials

◎ *Pat-A-Cake, Pat-A-Cake, Baker's Man* (page 115)

◎ *Pat-A-Cake, Pat-A-Cake, Baker's Man Word Ladder* (page 116)

◎ *Pat-A-Cake, Pat-A-Cake, Baker's Man Open Word Sort* (pages 117–118)

◎ *Pat-A-Cake, Pat-A-Cake, Baker's Man Rhyming Riddles* (page 119)

◎ *Pat-A-Cake, Pat-A-Cake, Baker's Man Reader's Theater* (pages 120–121)

◎ chart paper

Procedures

Introducing the Rhyme

1. Copy the rhyme onto a sheet of chart paper.

2. Read the rhyme to students using a pointer to track print.

3. Distribute the *Pat-A-Cake, Pat-A-Cake, Baker's Man* rhyme (page 115) to students.

4. Ask students to read the rhyme chorally from their own copies.

5. Encourage students to track print by pointing to individual words from the rhyme.

6. Teach students a hand-clapping game to accompany the rhythm of the rhyme.

7. Allow students to illustrate the rhyme and add it to their individual poetry notebooks.

8. Have students add the title to their notebooks' tables of contents.

Word Ladder

1. Distribute *Pat-A-Cake, Pat-A-Cake, Baker's Man Word Ladder* (page 116) to students.

2. Allow students time to observe the illustrations on their activity sheets.

3. After students have had time to review their activity sheets, tell them to follow your clues to make a word ladder from *pat* to *man*. Say the following:

   ◎ start at the bottom of the ladder—what the baker's man did to the cake (*pat*)

   ◎ change the first letter—an animal that is like a big mouse (*rat*)

   ◎ change the first letter—what you use to hit a ball (*bat*)

   ◎ change the first letter—the opposite of thin (*fat*)

   ◎ change the last letter—something that cools you off (*fan*)

   ◎ change the first letter—the person in the poem: baker's _____ (*man*)

4. Help students make a meaningful connection between the poem and the first and last rungs of the ladder.

Pat-A-Cake, Pat-A-Cake, Baker's Man (cont.)

Open Word Sort [color] [size] [shape]

1. Distribute sets of the *Pat-A-Cake, Pat-A-Cake, Baker's Man Open Word Sort* cards (pages 117–118) to individual students, pairs of students, or groups of students.

2. Read the words on the cards together.

3. Have students read the words and decide how they can be sorted.

4. Follow the sorting with a discussion of word meanings and the different ways word groups were created.

5. Discuss how the words relate to the rhyme.

Rhyming Riddles ???

1. Ask students to think of words that rhyme with the word *cake*. Have them share their words with partners.

2. Record their words on the board.

3. Distribute *Pat-A-Cake, Pat-A-Cake, Baker's Man Rhyming Riddles* (page 119) to students and make connections between the words that students come up with in Step 1 to the words in the Word Bank.

4. Instruct students to use words from the Word Bank to complete the riddles.

5. Have students illustrate one of the rhyming riddles on the backs of their papers.

Writing Connection

1. As a class, brainstorm a list of all alphabet letters that rhyme with the word *me* (e.g., *b, c, d, e, g, p, t, v, z*).

2. Have students use the list of letters to dictate a copy change of the last two lines of the rhyme, such as the following:

   > Roll it and roll it, and mark it with a *D*,
   >
   > And put it in the oven for Daddy and me.

   > Roll it and roll it, and mark it with *P*,
   >
   > And put it in the oven for puppy and me.

3. Record their verses on a sheet of chart paper.

4. Read the chart chorally.

Reader's Theater

1. You can approach the *Pat-A-Cake, Pat-A-Cake, Baker's Man Reader's Theater* script (pages 120–121) in a number of ways depending on the ability of your students and the time of year. You can change the number of readers depending on the approach you use. Consider using the following:

   ◎ Write the lines on sentence strips, and pass them out to students.

   ◎ Give students scripts and have them highlight their assigned parts.

   ◎ Give the script to older reading buddies to practice and perform for the kindergartners.

2. Allow several rehearsals to develop fluency.

3. Perform the reader's theater for the class, another class, or for a special school event.

Pat-A-Cake, Pat-A-Cake, Baker's Man

Traditional Rhyme

Pat-a-cake, pat-a-cake, baker's man.

Bake me a cake, as fast as you can;

Roll it and roll it, and mark it with *B*,

And put it in the oven for Bobby and me.

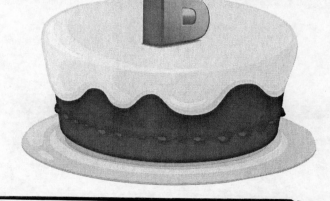

Name: _____

Pat-A-Cake, Pat-A-Cake, Baker's Man

Word Ladder

Directions: Listen to the clues. Then, write the words on the rungs below as you climb the ladder.

6. _man_

5. _____

4. _____

3. _____

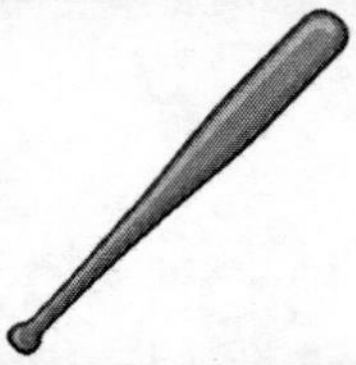

2. _____

1. _pat_

Pat-A-Cake, Pat-A-Cake, Baker's Man

Open Word Sort

Directions: Cut apart the cards. Then, sort them into groups that you choose. Be ready to explain your groups.

pat	man
mat	can
fan	bake
rat	cake
cat	tan

Pat-A-Cake, Pat-A-Cake, Baker's Man

Open Word Sort (cont.)

lake	rake
take	hat
bat	fat
sat	pan
ran	van

 #51336—Rhythm & Rhyme Literacy Time

Name: _____

Pat-A-Cake, Pat-A-Cake, Baker's Man
Rhyming Riddles

Directions: Use words from the Word Bank to complete the riddles about a cake.

Word Bank

fake   awake   bake   lake

1. cake that fell in the water

   _____

   cake in the _____

2. cake that isn't real

   _____

   cake that is _____

3. cake that you put in the oven

   _____

   cake that you _____

4. cake that is not asleep

   _____

   cake that is _____

Pat-A-Cake, Pat-A-Cake, Baker's Man
Reader's Theater

All: Pat-A-Cake, Pat-A-Cake Baker's Man

Reader 1: I never knew you could pat a cake.

Reader 2: My mom makes cakes, but she never pats them. She just mixes them and puts them in a pan to bake.

Reader 3: Maybe it was a special kind of cake.

Reader 4: Maybe it was more like cookie dough.

Reader 5: You could pat cookie dough.

Reader 1: You could also roll cookie dough like it says in the rhyme.

Reader 2: So the cake was really a big cookie that was patted and rolled and baked.

Pat-A-Cake, Pat-A-Cake, Baker's Man
Reader's Theater (cont.)

Reader 3: It was marked with a *B* before they baked it.

Reader 4: *B* was for Bobby and me.

Reader 1: I am going to ask my mom to make me a big cookie like that with my name on it.

Reader 5: Maybe you could ask her to bake a really big one and mark it with a *C*.

Reader 2: What is the *C* for?

Reader 5: *C* means for the whole class.

Readers 1–4: Good idea!

There Was an Old Woman Lived Under a Hill

Standards

◎ Isolate and pronounce the initial, medial vowel, and final sounds (phonemes) in three-phoneme words.

◎ Add or substitute individual sounds in simple, one-syllable words to make new words.

◎ See Appendix C for additional standards.

Materials

◎ *There Was an Old Woman Lived Under a Hill* (page 124)

◎ *Letter Cards* (page 132)

◎ *There Was an Old Woman Lived Under a Hill Closed Word Sort* (page 125)

◎ *There Was an Old Woman Lived Under a Hill Rhyming Riddles* (page 126)

◎ *There Was an Old Woman Lived Under a Hill Reader's Theater* (pages 127–128)

◎ chart paper

◎ online illustration of the rhyme *(optional)*

Procedures

Introducing the Rhyme

1. Copy the rhyme onto a sheet of chart paper.

2. Read the rhyme to students using a pointer to track print.

3. If desired, look online to find an illustration of the rhyme. Show students the illustration, and discuss the meaning of "lived under a hill."

4. Distribute the *There Was an Old Woman Lived Under a Hill* rhyme (page 124) to students.

5. Read the rhyme chorally as you track print on the chart.

6. Ask students to help you count how many words are in each line.

7. Allow students to illustrate the rhyme and add it to their individual poetry notebooks.

8. Have students add the title to their notebooks' tables of contents.

Change a Word

1. Distribute a set of *Letter Cards* (page 132) to each student. If this activity is used early in the year, we recommend you use only the letters they will need (*o, l, d, o, g, u, u, t, p, b, n, e*).

2. Before you begin the activity, have students identify the letters and corresponding sounds.

3. Allow students time to arrange the letters to make their own words.

4. After students have had time to make and share words, ask them to put the letters in a pile and follow your instructions. Say the following:

   ◎ We will make a word that is in the rhyme. Use three letters to make the word *old*. What letters did you use? (*o, l, d*)

   ◎ We will make a new word by starting with the last letter in *old*. What is the last letter in *old*? Make a word that starts with *d* and means an animal that barks. What letters did you add? What word did you make? (*dog*)

There Was an Old Woman Lived Under a Hill (cont.)

Change a Word (cont.) abc

- We will make a new word by starting with the last letter in *dog*. What is the last letter in dog? Make a word that starts with *g* that is the opposite of *come*. What letter did you add? What word did you make? (*go*)

- Let's make a new word that starts with the last letter in *go*. What is the last letter in go? Make a word that is the opposite of *in*. What letters did you add? What word did you make? (*out*)

- Start with the last letter of *out*. What is the last letter of *out*? Make a word that is the opposite of *bottom*. What letters did you add? What word did you make? (*top*)

- Keep all your letters, but rearrange them to make another word for *pan*. What word did you make? (*pot*)

- Start with the last letter in *pot*. What is the last letter in *pot*? Make a word that tells where you take a bath. What letters did you add? What word did you make? (*tub*)

- Start with the last letter in *tub*. What is the last letter in *tub*? Make a word that we sometimes use for an insect. What letters did you add? What word did you make? (*bug*)

- Let's do one more word. Make a new word by starting with the last letter in *bug*. What is the last letter in *bug*? Make a word from the rhyme that goes in this blank:

> There was an old woman
>
> Lived under a hill,
>
> And if she's not _____
>
> She lives there still

What letters did you add? What word did you make? (*gone*)

Closed Word Sort color size shape

1. Distribute sets of the *There Was an Old Woman Lived Under a Hill Closed Word Sort* cards (page 125) to individual students, pairs of students, or groups of students.

2. Ask students to put words into groups according to whether they rhyme or do not rhyme.

3. Follow the sorting with a discussion of rhyming words in the poem.

Rhyming Riddles ???

1. Ask students to think of words that rhyme with the word *hill*. Have them share their words with partners.

2. Record their words on the board.

3. Distribute *There Was an Old Woman Lived Under a Hill Rhyming Riddles* (page 126) to students and make connections between the words that students come up with in Step 1 to the words in the Word Bank.

4. Instruct students to use words from the Word Bank to complete the riddles.

5. Have students illustrate one of the rhyming riddles on the backs of their papers.

Writing Connection

1. Have students write lists of other places the old woman might live. Encourage developmental spelling.

2. Have students share their lists with partners.

Reader's Theater

1. Distribute the *There Was an Old Woman Lived Under a Hill Reader's Theater* script (pages 127–128) to students.

2. Assign parts for five readers.

3. Allow several rehearsals to develop fluency.

4. Perform the reader's theater for the class, another class, or for a special school event.

There Was an Old Woman Lived Under a Hill

Traditional Rhyme

There was an old woman
Lived under a hill,
And if she's not gone
She lives there still.

Baked apples she sold
And cranberry pies,
And she's the
  old woman
Who never told lies.

There Was an Old Woman Lived Under a Hill

Closed Word Sort

Directions: Cut apart the cards. Then, sort them into two groups: words that rhyme and words that do not rhyme.

tin	lie
pie	pack
fly	cry
eye	lane
lip	tie

Name: _____

There Was an Old Woman Lived Under a Hill
Rhyming Riddles

Directions: Use words from the Word Bank to complete the riddles about the old woman.

Word Bank

bill	Jill	fill	pill

1. She is sick.

_____

She needs a _____ .

2. She knows Jack and his sister.

_____

She knows _____ .

3. The old woman needs a bucket full of water.

_____

She needs to _____ her bucket.

4. The old woman has a duck with a beak.

_____

She has a duck with a _____ .

There Was an Old Woman Lived Under a Hill

Reader's Theater

All: There Was an Old Woman Lived Under a Hill

Reader 1: I know an old woman who lived in a tent.

Reader 2: Why did she live in a tent?

Reader 1: She liked to hear the night sounds as she slept.

Reader 3: What kinds of night sounds?

Reader 4: Maybe she liked to hear the crickets chirp.

Reader 5: Or maybe she liked to hear the owls hoot.

Reader 2: What about in the winter?

Reader 1: I think she lived in her house in the winter.

There Was an Old Woman Lived Under a Hill

Reader's Theater (cont.)

Reader 3: It would be too cold to live in a tent in the winter.

Reader 4: My friend said that her grandmother lives at the airport.

Reader 5: Nobody is allowed to live at the airport.

Reader 4: My friend said that when they miss her grandmother, they go to the airport and pick her up. Then, when she's ready to go home, they take her back to the airport.

Reader 5: That just means that her grandmother lives far away and takes a plane to visit them.

Reader 4: I will tell my friend.

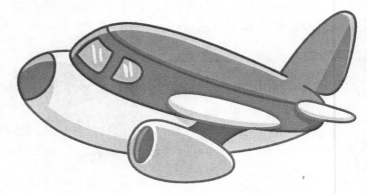

Tips for Implementing the Lessons

The Importance of Routines

Reading instruction needs to include a measure of predictability through activities that students do at regular times in their language arts classroom. Routines allow students to become self-directed learners because once they learn the routine, they do not have to rely on the teacher for directions for what to do next. This increases students' learning time and decreases teachers' planning time (Rasinski and Padak 2013; Rasinski, Padak, and Fawcett 2010).

Each lesson in this book follows a routine:

1. Introduction, Reading, and Rereading of the Rhyme

2. Word Work activities
   → *Word Ladder* or *Change a Word*
   → *Word Sort* or *Yes and No*
   → *Rhyming Riddles*

3. Writing Connection

4. Reader's Theater

The intention is not that you march sequentially through all the rhymes and activities in this book. Use the standards that accompany each lesson to guide you in selecting the rhymes and activities that your students need at any given time. Some standards may be addressed adequately in other instructional materials you use, while you may find some gaps in your curriculum that can be filled with activities in this book. In addition to the standards, stay attuned to what your students enjoy and learn from most.

Each lesson has multiple activities, so even if you eliminate a few, you will not be able to complete an entire lesson in one day. The following one-week routine can be adjusted according to the number of activities you decide to use. Another option is to learn the rhymes early in the year, revisit them regularly, and do an activity each time you revisit them.

Day	Task
Day 1	Introduce the rhyme to students.
Day 2	Reread the rhyme and complete one of the word work activities.
Day 3	Assign and practice the reader's theater script and complete a second word work activity.
Day 4	Practice the reader's theater script and complete the last word work activity.
Day 5	Perform the reader's theater script and complete the writing connection activity.

Tips for Implementing the Lessons *(cont.)*

Differentiation

We have been in education long enough to know that, despite frequent attempts at standardizing curriculum, instruction, and assessment, there is no such thing as a "standardized" child. Children in our schools come with great differences in abilities, background experiences, and motivation to learn. Perhaps nowhere are the differences as obvious as they are in our nation's kindergarten classes. We are aware that the students of kindergarten teachers who use this book will range from children who have had little experience with print to children who are already reading when they begin school.

Each lesson begins with the class orally reading a rhyme or poem. If most of your students come to school reading or nearly ready to read, they may be familiar with many of the rhymes already. In that case, you will find the reader's theater scripts a good extension of the rhymes as well as an excellent source of reading material.

If you mainly teach children who have little knowledge of concepts of print, know few letters and sounds, and need to develop phonemic awareness, you may want to spend time just getting familiar with the nursery rhymes and save the reader's theater scripts for later in the year. You also might consider establishing reading buddies from a higher grade level to take on the reader's theater component of the lessons initially. Kindergartners could recite the rhyme for their reading buddies, and the older reading buddies could perform the reader's theater script for the kindergartners. You could also send your students and their reading buddies in teams to perform for other classes.

Your class may consist of children who need a great deal of readiness work as well as emergent readers and proficient readers. Choral reading of the rhymes will allow the more fluent readers to provide support for their less fluent classmates. It is a wonderful way to build group spirit and cohesion. Don't worry if some students seem to be "memorizing" rather than actually reading the words. Although in past years students were discouraged from using their fingers to point to words, we now know this is an appropriate strategy for children just learning to read, so encourage students to track print with their fingers, and before long the memorized words will become part of their reading vocabulary.

Your students may be able to use developmental spelling to complete the Writing Connection activities or they may need to dictate their responses to you for a while. As with any instructional material, there is no one thing in this book that will work for all children all the time. Your professional knowledge and experience will guide you in selecting which parts of the lessons you should use.

Tips for Implementing the Lessons *(cont.)*

Poetry Notebooks

Poetry Notebooks are an effective and engaging way to help students learn to recognize the form and sound of poetry. After the initial introduction of a poem or rhyme, students are given copies of it that they illustrate and add to three-ring binders.

Throughout the year, students enjoy browsing their poetry notebooks during sustained silent reading, reading poems with partners during independent reading time, and sharing the poems with family and friends. A table of contents will help students locate their favorites. Some teachers add a "Lucky Listener" sheet to the front of the poetry notebook. Students take the notebooks home on a regular basis, and anyone they read to signs the sheet and makes comments if they wish. Some children even read to their pets and sign it themselves ("Good job! Love, Goldie") or make a paw print in the signature space. To help your students create poetry notebooks, see pages 134–136 for the *My Poetry Notebook* cover, the *Table of Contents*, and the *Lucky Listener* page.

Letter Cards

Teacher Directions: Copy and cut apart the cards. Distribute sets to students. **Note:** Read Step 1 in all *Change a Word* activities to see if you need to write additional letters on the empty cards.

a	b	c	d	e
f	g	h	i	j
k	l	m	n	o
p	q	r	s	t
u	v	w	x	y
z				

Name: _____

My Rhyming Words

Words that rhyme with _____

_____   _____

_____   _____

_____   _____

_____   _____

_____   _____

_____   _____

My Poetry Notebook

by _____

Table of Contents

Title   **Page**

_____   _____

_____   _____

_____   _____

_____   _____

_____   _____

_____   _____

_____   _____

_____   _____

_____   _____

_____   _____

_____   _____

_____   _____

Lucky Listener

You have been chosen to be a Lucky Listener! You have the privilege of listening to _____ read the poems in his or her notebook. Please "autograph" below. Feel free to add comments. Enjoy!

Name	Comments
_____	_____
_____	_____
_____	_____
_____	_____
_____	_____
_____	_____
_____	_____
_____	_____
_____	_____
_____	_____
_____	_____
_____	_____
_____	_____

Standards Correlations

Shell Education is committed to producing educational materials that are research and standards based. In this effort, we have correlated all of our products to the academic standards of all 50 states, the District of Columbia, the Department of Defense Dependents Schools, and all Canadian provinces.

How to Find Standards Correlations

To print a customized correlation report of this product for your state, visit our website at http://www.shelleducation.com and follow the on-screen directions. If you require assistance in printing correlation reports, please contact our Customer Service Department at 1-877-777-3450.

Purpose and Intent of Standards

Legislation mandates that all states adopt academic standards that identify the skills students will learn in kindergarten through grade twelve. Many states also have standards for Pre–K. This same legislation sets requirements to ensure the standards are detailed and comprehensive.

Standards are designed to focus instruction and guide adoption of curricula. Standards are statements that describe the criteria necessary for students to meet specific academic goals. They define the knowledge, skills, and content students should acquire at each level. Standards are also used to develop standardized tests to evaluate students' academic progress. Teachers are required to demonstrate how their lessons meet state standards. State standards are used in the development of all of our products, so educators can be assured they meet the academic requirements of each state.

Common Core State Standards

The activities in this book are aligned to the Common Core State Standards (CCSS). The chart on pages 138–141 lists the standards addressed in each lesson. Specific standards are also listed on the first page of each lesson.

TESOL and WIDA Standards

The activities in this book promote English language development for English language learners. The following TESOL and WIDA standards are addressed through the activities in this book:

◎ **Standard 1:** English language learners **communicate** for **social**, **intercultural**, and **instructional** purposes within the school setting.

◎ **Standard 2:** English language learners **communicate** information, ideas, and concepts necessary for academic success in the area of **language arts**.

Standards Correlations *(cont.)*

Standards that are specific to lessons are included on the first pages of the lesson and in the chart below. Standards that fit every lesson are listed below and indicate All Lessons. They are not always indicated on the first pages of the lessons.

Common Core State Standards	Lessons
Literacy.L.K.1—With prompting and support, ask and answer questions about key details in a text.	All Lessons
Literacy.L.K.1.a—Print many upper- and lowercase letters.	All Lessons
Literacy.L.K.1.c—Form regular, plural nouns orally by adding /s/ or /es/.	Hark! Hark! (p. 72)
Literacy.L.K.2—With prompting and support, retell familiar stories, including key details.	All Lessons
Literacy.L.K.2.a—Capitalize the first word in a sentence and the pronoun *I*.	Handy-Spandy, Jack-A-Dandy (p. 106)
Literacy.L.K.2.b—Recognize and name end punctuation.	Hark! Hark! (p. 72); Handy-Spandy, Jack-A-Dandy (p. 106)
Literacy.L.K.2.c—Write a letter or letters for most consonant and short-vowel sounds (phonemes).	All Lessons
Literacy.L.K.2.d—Spell simple words phonetically, drawing on knowledge of sound-letter relationships.	All Lessons
Literacy.L.K.3—With prompting and support, identify characters, settings, and major events in a story.	All Lessons
Literacy.L.K.4—Determine or clarify the meaning of unknown and multiple-meaning words and phrases based on kindergarten reading and content.	Row, Row, Row Your Boat (p. 9); Baa, Baa, Black Sheep (p. 23); Shoe Goo (p. 31); The Fly (p. 47); To Market (p. 55); Itsy Bitsy Spider (p. 63); Hark! Hark! (p. 72); Diddle, Diddle, Dumpling (p. 81); Molly, Molly (p. 98); Handy-Spandy, Jack-A-Dandy (p. 106)
Literacy.L.K.5—Recognize common types of texts (e.g., storybooks, poems).	All Lessons
Literacy.L.K.5.a—Sort common objects into categories (e.g., shapes, foods) to gain a sense of the concepts the categories represent.	All Lessons

Standards Correlations *(cont.)*

Common Core State Standards	Lessons
Literacy.L.K.6—Use words and phrases acquired through conversations, reading and being read to, and responding to texts.	All Lessons
Literacy.L.K.10—Actively engage in group reading activities with purpose and understanding.	All Lessons
Literacy.RF.K.1.a—Follow words from left to right, top to bottom, and page by page.	All Lessons
Literacy.RF.K.2—Demonstrate understanding of spoken words, syllables, and sounds (phonemes).	All Lessons
Literacy.RF.K.2.a—Recognize and produce rhyming words.	All Lessons
Literacy.RF.K.2.b—Count, pronounce, blend, and segment syllables in spoken words.	Polly, Put the Kettle On (p. 16); The Fly (p. 47); Itsy Bitsy Spider (p. 63); Molly, Molly (p. 98)
Literacy.RF.K.2.c—Blend and segment onsets and rimes of single-syllable spoken words.	Row, Row, Row Your Boat (p. 9)
Literacy.RF.K.2.d—Isolate and pronounce the initial, medial vowel, and final sounds (phonemes) in three-phoneme (consonant-vowel-consonant, or CVC) words.	Itsy Bitsy Spider (p. 63); My Dog Joe (p. 89); Molly, Molly (p. 98); Handy-Spandy, Jack-A-Dandy (p. 106); Pat-A-Cake, Pat-A-Cake, Baker's Man (p. 113); There Was an Old Woman Lived Under a Hill (p. 122)
Literacy.RF.K.2.e—Add or substitute individual sounds (phonemes) in simple, one-syllable words to make new words.	Baa, Baa, Black Sheep (p. 23); My Dog Joe (p. 89); Handy-Spandy, Jack-A-Dandy (p. 106); Pat-A-Cake, Pat-A-Cake, Baker's Man (p. 113); There Was an Old Woman Lived Under a Hill (p. 122)
Literacy.RF.K.3—Know and apply grade-level phonics and word analysis skills in decoding words.	All Lessons
Literacy.RF.K.3.a—Demonstrate basic knowledge of one-to-one letter-sound correspondences by producing the primary or many of the most frequent sounds for each consonant.	Polly, Put the Kettle On (p. 16); One, Two Buckle My Shoe (p. 38); The Fly (p. 47); To Market (p. 55); Molly, Molly (p. 98); Pat-A-Cake, Pat-A-Cake, Baker's Man (p. 113)

Standards Correlations *(cont.)*

Common Core State Standards	Lessons
Literacy.RF.K.3.b—Associate the long and short sounds with common spellings (graphemes) for the five major vowels.	One, Two, Buckle My Shoe (p. 38); To Market (p. 55)
Literacy.RF.K.3.c—Read common high-frequency words by sight.	All Lessons
Literacy.RF.K.4—Read emergent-reader texts with purpose and understanding.	All Lessons
Literacy.RI.K.2—With prompting and support, identify the main topic and retell key details of a text.	Shoe Goo (p. 31)
Literacy.W.K.5—With guidance and support from adults, respond to questions and suggestions from peers and add details to strengthen writing as needed.	My Dog Joe (p. 89)
Literacy.RL.K.4—Ask and answer questions about unknown words in a text.	All Lessons
Literacy.RF.1—Demonstrate understanding of the organization and basic features of print.	All Lessons
Literacy.RF.1.b—Recognize that spoken words are represented in written language by specific sequences of letters.	All Lessons
Literacy.RF.1.c—Understand that words are separated by spaces in print.	All Lessons
Literacy.SL.K.1—Participate in collaborative conversations with diverse partners about *kindergarten topics and texts* with peers and adults in small and larger groups.	All Lessons
Literacy.SL.K.1.a—Follow agreed-upon rules for discussions (e.g., listening to others and taking turns speaking about the topics and texts under discussion).	All Lessons
Literacy.SL.K.1.b—Continue a conversation through multiple exchanges.	All Lessons

Standards Correlations (cont.)

Common Core State Standards	Lessons
Literacy.SL.K.2—Confirm understanding of a text read aloud or information presented orally or through other media by asking and answering questions about key details and requesting clarification if something is not understood.	All Lessons
Literacy.SL.K.6—Speak audibly and express thoughts, feelings, and ideas clearly.	All Lessons
Literacy.L.K.1—With prompting and support, ask and answer questions about key details in a text.	All Lessons
Literacy.L.K.1.a—Print many upper- and lowercase letters.	All Lessons
Literacy.L.K.1.d—Understand and use question words (e.g., *who, what, where, when, why, how*).	Diddle, Diddle, Dumpling (p. 81)

References Cited

Adams, Marilyn J. 1990. *Beginning to Read: Thinking and Learning About Print*. Cambridge, MA: MIT Press.

Ball, Eileen, and Benita A. Blachman. 1991. "Does Phoneme Awareness Training in Kindergarten Make a Difference in Early Word Recognition and Developmental Spelling?" *Reading Research Quarterly* 26: 49–66.

Bromley, Karen. 2007. "Nine Things Every Teacher Should Know About Words and Vocabulary Instruction." *Journal of Adolescent and Adult Literacy* 50: 528–537.

Bryant, Peter E., Lynette Bradley, Morag Maclean, and Jennifer Crossland. 1989. "Nursery Rhymes, Phonological Skills, and Reading." *Journal of Child Language* 16 (2): 407–428.

Chall, Jeanne. 1983. *Stages of Reading Development*. New York, NY: McGraw Hill.

Denman, Gregory A. 1988. *When You've Made it Your Own: Teaching Poetry to Young People*. Portsmouth, NH: Heinemann.

Dowhower, Sarah L. 1987. "Effects of Repeated Reading on Second-Grade Transitional Readers' Fluency and Comprehension." *Reading Research Quarterly* 22: 389–407.

———. 1997. "The Method of Repeated Readings." *The Reading Teacher* 50: 376.

Dunst, Carl, Diana Meter, and Deborah W. Hornby. 2011. "Relationship Between Young Children's Nursery Rhyme Experiences and Knowledge and Phonological and Print-Related Abilities." *Center for Early Literacy Learning* 4: 1–12.

Gill, Sharon R. 2011. "The Forgotten Genre of Children's Poetry." *The Reading Teacher* 60: 622–625.

Griffith, Priscilla L., and Janell P. Klesius. 1990. "The Effect of Phonemic Awareness Ability and Reading Instructional Approach on First Grade Children's Acquisition of Spelling and Decoding Skills." Paper presented at the annual meeting of the National Reading Conference, Miami, FL.

Hackett, Kelly. 2013. *Ready! Set! Go! Literacy Centers*. Huntington Beach, CA: Shell Education.

Iwasaki, Becky, Timothy V. Rasinski, Kasim Yildirim, and Belinda S. Zimmerman. 2013. "Let's Bring Back the Magic of Song for Teaching Reading." *The Reading Teacher* 67: 137–141.

Maclean, Morag, Peter Bryant, and Lynette Bradley. 1987. "Rhymes, Nursery Rhymes, and Reading in Early Childhood." *Merrill Palmer Quarterly* 33: 255–281.

National Reading Panel. 2000. "Report of the National Reading Panel: Teaching Children to Read." Report of the subgroups. Washington, DC: U.S. Department of Health and Human Services, National Institutes of Health.

Perfect, Kathy A. 1999. "Rhyme and Reason: Poetry for the Heart and Head." *The Reading Teacher* 5: 728–737.

Rasinski, Timothy V., and Nancy D. Padak. 2013. *From Phonics to Fluency: Effective Teaching of Decoding and Reading Fluency in the Elementary School*. Boston, MA: Pearson.

References Cited *(cont.)*

Rasinski, Timothy V., Nancy D. Padak, and Gay Fawcett. 2010. *Teaching Children Who Find Reading Difficult, 4th ed.* Boston, MA: Pearson.

Rasinski, Timothy V., Nancy D. Padak, Elizabeth Sturtevant, and Wayne Linek. 1994. "Effects of Fluency Development on Urban Second-Grade Readers." *Journal of Educational Research* 87: 158–165.

Rasinski, Timothy V., William H. Rupley, and William D. Nichols. 2008. "Two Essential Ingredients: Phonics and Fluency Getting to Know Each Other." *The Reading Teacher* 62: 257–260.

———. 2012. *Phonics and Fluency Practice with Poetry.* New York: Scholastic.

Rasinski, Timothy V., and Belinda Zimmerman. 2013. "What's the Perfect Text for Struggling Readers? Try Poetry!" *Reading Today* 30: 15–16.

Samuels, S. Jay. 1997. "The Method of Repeated Readings." *The Reading Teacher* 50: 376–381.

Seitz, Sheila K. 2013. "Poetic Fluency." *The Reading Teacher* 67: 312–14.

Stahl, Steven A. 2003. "Vocabulary and Readability: How Knowing Word Meanings Affects Comprehension." *Topics in Language Disorders* 23 (3): 241–248.

Stahl, Steven A., and Kathleen M. Heubach. 2005. "Fluency-Oriented Reading Instruction." *Journal of Literacy Research* 37: 25–60.

Stanovich, Keith E. 1994. "Romance and Reason." *The Reading Teacher* 49: 280–291.

Templeton, Shane, and Donald Bear. 2011. "Teaching Phonemic Awareness, Spelling, and Word Recognition." In *Rebuilding the Foundation: Effective Reading Instruction for the 21st Century,* edited by Timothy Rasinski 1–10. Bloomington, IN: Solution Tree.

Zimmerman, Belinda, and Timothy V. Rasinski. 2012. "The Fluency Development Lesson: A Model of Authentic and Effective Fluency Instruction." In *Fluency Instruction* 2nd ed., edited by Timothy V. Rasinski, Camille Blachowicz, and Kristin Lems, 172–184. New York, NY: Guilford.

Zimmerman, Belinda, Timothy V. Rasinski, and Maria Melewski. 2013. "When Kids Can't Read, What a Focus on Fluency Can Do." In *Advanced Literacy Practices: From the Clinic to the Classroom,* edited by Evan Ortlieb and Earl H. Cheek, 137–160. Bingley, UK: Emerald Group Publishing.